WILD AT HEА

THE SOUTH ISLAND'S WEST COAST

PADDY RYAN

EXISLE
PUBLISHING

NEW ZEALAND BEHIND THE POSTCARDS

Dedicated to Felicity, Sarah and Lucy
for their love, friendship and support.

(Above) **For many decades steam locomotives were a familiar sight and sound on the coastal strip and river valleys north of Hokitika.** (Front Cover) **Blowhole action at Truman Track, Paparoa National Park, during a westerly swell.** (Inside Front Cover) **The Hokitika Gorge is one of the West Coast's unsung attractions. A short walk through native bush leads to a suspension bridge over blue glacial melt water.** (Right) **The Gates of Haast bridge. Earlier bridges were swept away by torrential flooding.** (Back Cover) **Kekeno, New Zealand fur seals resting on rocks near Arnott Point, South Westland. Once hunted to the verge of extinction, these animals are now making a comeback.**

ISBN 0-908988-01-X

First published in New Zealand in 1994 by
Exisle Publishing Ltd
PO Box 8077, Auckland,
New Zealand.

Printed by Colorcraft Ltd, Hong Kong.

Typeset in Berkeley, Caslon Openface and Frutiger
by Streamline Graphic Imaging Ltd, Auckland.

Photographs by Paddy Ryan

Designed by Craig Humberstone.

Publication of this book was assisted by Westland Brewery (brewer of Monteith's),
whose support is gratefully acknowledged.

Acknowledgements:
Thanks to the following people for their help with this book: Jenny Barratt, John Benn, Mike Browne, Allan Coll, John Crawford, John Daniel, Kirsten Disse, Peter Fairhall, Des Heaphy, Denise Howard, Keri Hulme, Monica Hulme, Tony and Raewi Ibbotson, Claudia Landis, Bob McKerrow, Gerry McSweeney, Phillipa Newman, Damien O'Connor, Felicity Ryan, Anne Saunders, Paul Schramm, Iri and Tamai Sinclair, David Stapleton, Bruce Stuart-Menteath, Doug Truman, Chris Weaver, Ian Wooster.

CONTENTS

Introduction	4
The Land	7
Poutini Ngai Tahu	8
Gold	22
Coal	27
Forests & Forestry	30
Sphagnum	32
The Animals	42
The Kotuku	48
The Coasters	54
The Potters	58
Sports & Leisure	64
Nature Tourism	66
Information Finder	70
Calendar	70
Suggested Reading	70
Map	71
Heading West	72

"IT'S THE LOVE OF THE LAND AND THE WARMTH OF THE PEOPLE."

(Above) **Alpine tarn, South Westland.**
(Right) **Wood chopper competing at Moana centennial celebrations, 1993: a big-hearted people inhabiting an alluring landscape of the mind.**

FROM an early age, New Zealanders are brought up on West Coast stories. There is nowhere else in the country which rivals the region for mystique. Even people who live on the west coast of the North Island recognise that the "real" West Coast lies further south, in and adjacent to the province of Westland. For anyone familiar with the people and places of Aotearoa, the West Coast looms larger than life.

This is an impressive tribute to Coasters and to the alluring country they inhabit. The West Coast is more a state of mind rather than a physical entity. While it is possible to say that the West Coast stretches from Kahurangi Point to Awarua Point, the boundaries are quite elastic. On a good day, if you're driving from Canterbury, the West Coast starts around Darfield rather than Arthur's Pass.

But officialdom can't cope with areas which are determined by your state of mind; they require real boundaries. Reluctantly these are included in the map but you don't really need them. There are parts of the West Coast in Auckland, Wellington, Christchurch and Dunedin. Many of these expatriate Coasters still celebrate St Patrick's Day in the style to which they are accustomed. The preferred brew is Monteith's, enthusiastically prepared in Greymouth with West Coast water and shipped elsewhere. Expat Coasters still cook whitebait patties from the supply sent "over the hill" by friends and relatives.

This is not to suggest that all 33,000 Coasters live in peace, love and harmony. The rivalry between towns is intense. At times this enmity leads the uninitiated to believe that Coasters are split on geographic lines. For example, Coastcare, the West Coast hospital and health authority, recently closed an antiquated X-ray machine in Hokitika. Residents of Hokitika and further south were faced with driving the extra half-hour to Greymouth. Coastcare made its decision on economic grounds and offered to provide a free taxi service. It made no difference; there was an immediate outcry in Hokitika and relative silence in Greymouth. Hokitika has the airport, Greymouth the Tranz-Alpine Express, Westport the port. Hokitika has the dairy factory, Greymouth the brewery, Westport the cement works, and so it goes.

However it requires only the threat of some form of intervention from "away" for Coasters to unite. It comes as no surprise that the New Zealand Trade Union movement and the Labour Party had their genesis on the Coast. The user-pays philosophies so loved by the new right hold little appeal for the people of this region. Despite their rugged individualism, West Coasters are probably the most public-spirited citizens in the country.

The appeal of the West Coast is the same for Coasters as it is for visitors. It's the love of the land and the warmth of the people. The isolation and the sense of history are almost palpable. West Coasters are proud of their past and enjoy celebrating the old days.

Before the arrival of the pakeha, Maori ranged widely over the Coast. It was their only source of pounamu or greenstone (jade or nephrite). Pounamu was held in high esteem for its hardness and the sharpness of the edges which could be lovingly fashioned from it. Pounamu was more than just a resource to Maori. It still holds mystical associations for them and they go to great lengths to recover it (see sidebar on Maori).

The record of Maori occupation of the Coast is incomplete, but what evidence there is, suggests that they first arrived around 800 years ago and have been here ever since.

In the mid-1800s the Coast was the scene of a rich and prolonged gold rush, the legacy of which is still with us. As the gold began to run out, other extractive industries were developed and a long association with coal and timber began. These industries have left their mark throughout the Coast and provide the basis for many interesting historical sites.

Unless you were born here you can't be considered a Coaster, but you can be accorded honorary Coaster status. This could involve a long wait. At a recent public dairy farming forum, the Chairman referred to a "Canterbury farmer who lives down the road; he's been here 30 years".

FELICITY RYAN

(Above) **The Hokitika Wild Foods Festival showcases many kinds of local talent.**
(Left) **Whitebaiter Bert Love waits on the banks of the Waitangiroto River in South Westland with his trusty scoop net.**

THE LAND

"I really enjoy it. I'd rather live here than over the hill. I used to live over the hill and it's a real jungle over there. I reckon it's safer here."

— Katherine Findlater, caretaker, Mokihinui.

MANY visitors to the Coast have very strange ideas about the geography of the place. One Education Department official on a visit to Reefton wanted to know if he could drive to Haast and back and still make his afternoon flight from Hokitika. Driving at the legal limit this trip would normally take around nine hours. Thin though the Coast may be, it is also exceedingly long. Coasters take delight in reminding visitors that the north-south distance is about the same as that from Auckland to Wellington.

It's a huge expanse and the relative inaccessibility of much of the interior makes it seem even larger. As it is, the Coast accounts for approximately eight percent of New Zealand's land area.

POUTINI NGAI TAHU

LIVING IN THE PRESENCE OF POUNAMU

T HE West Coast, Te Tai Poutini, holds great spiritual significance for Maori because of the presence of pounamu (greenstone, a form of nephrite or jade). Poutini, a taniwha (monster) which swims up and down the West Coast, is the guardian of both the people of the West Coast and the spiritual essence of pounamu.

Once, while in the North Island, Poutini abducted Waitaiki, the wife of Tamahua. Tamahua discovered the abduction in time to pursue Poutini on his journey south. Poutini took refuge from the pursuit up the Arahura River but Tamahua detected his presence and prepared to do battle.

Trapped, Poutini realised that he had little chance of escape but could not bear to leave the beautiful Waitaiki. Reasoning that if he couldn't have her, no-one else could either, he turned her into his own essence... pounamu. Then he travelled back down the river, successfully avoiding the distraught Tamahua. Poutini reached the coast safely and has subsequently been the kaitiaki or guardian of Te Tai Poutini and the precious stone it holds.

Waitaiki became the motherlode of pounamu.

Greenstone was the hardest and most durable material known to the Maori. It could be cut only with a type of quartzose slate. The work required patience. Just producing a roughly triangular block a few centimetres thick would take a month. Grinding it into its final shape, using a gritty sandstone, could take six weeks or even longer. According to Brailsford (in *The Tattooed Land, the Southern Frontiers of the Pa Maori*), Maori also discovered that relatively soft pre-nephrite could be converted into nephrite by heating to 650°C. Higher temperatures degraded the structure so it was a skilled undertaking.

The West Coast Maori developed trade with east coast tribes, bartering finished pounamu products for food and other items. It is unlikely that much food actually made it back over the Alps. This was the first of many extractive industries based on the Coast. These early trading trips utilised the Taramakau Pass and other passes including the Whitcombe, although the latter became tapu after a trading group perished in a blizzard.

West Coast Maori would make the hazardous journey to Milford Sound where they quarried tangiwai (bowenite), a soft translucent green stone that made excellent fish hooks or ornaments but was useless for tools as it was too soft to hold an edge for long.

There has been Maori habitation on the West Coast for around 800 years, yet archaeological records remain far from complete. This may be due to the limited amount of archaeological investigation or seasonal settlement patterns. Few permanent settlements are known. Pa sites (fortified villages)

(Left) **Maori with waka exploring on the Pororari River during filming of BBC's** *Nomads of the Wind* **series.** (Top) **Maori actor in traditional clothing for** *Nomads* **scene.** (Lower) **A greenstone tiki, carved many generations ago on the West Coast. It has now "gone home" because its owner has moved back to the Coast.**

(Top) **A tangiwai (bowenite) fish hook carved on the Coast from the mother-lode in Milford Sound.** (Lower) **A contemporary greenstone carving by acclaimed West Coast carver Ian Boustridge. Similar work can be viewed at The Jade Boulder Gallery in Greymouth.**

are known from only a few places and may reflect lower population pressure and less competition for resources than in other parts of the country. The most important pa were near Kawatiri, Mawhera (Greymouth), Arahura and Okarito. In recent years Jackson Bay has provided a wealth of artifacts but as yet no sign of a pa.

Much of European knowledge of West Coast Maori stems from the descriptions made by the early explorers. Surveyor and artist Charles Heaphy made the following observations about Taramakau Maori:

"They fish in the shallow parts of the Teramakau and Mawhera rivers in the summer, catching eels, soles, and white bait, the first of which they preserve in fat, potted in the bladder of the seaweed termed kelp. There are no canoes large enough to proceed to sea, and the only salt-water fish they obtain are sharks, from Potokihua. In the summer they catch great quantities of kakas, pigeons, and wekas. It is probably the worst off community in New Zealand, but the natives in no way seem dissatisfied with their condition. They appear more healthy generally than the natives elsewhere, and the comparative number of children is also greater. The absence of the blanket undoubtedly tends to their health, and here are to be met with no cases of pulmonary disease, which is so prevalent elsewhere. The absence of tabacco may also have a sanatory influence."

Charles Heaphy, 1846. In *The Tattooed Land, the Southern Frontiers of the Pa Maori* by Barry Brailsford.

Modern Maori obtain some rent from businesses in Greymouth which are built on their land. In most respects their lifestyle is very little different from the West Coast Europeans although traditional pursuits are still followed in an active attempt to maintain a sense of identity in an increasingly pakeha world. These include bone and pounamu carving, weaving using the coastal plants pingao, the climber kie kie and harakeke (flax) as well as singing and dancing.

In recent years there has been a resurgence in Maoritanga (Maori culture) as Maori throughout New Zealand come to grips with the changes wrought by the coming of the European. The Maori of the 1990s is an assertive, proud individual, determined to retain those elements of his or her culture which give them their identity and sense of purpose.

The ruggedness of the region is easily explained. The West Coast straddles the Alpine fault, a ruler-straight division between two quite distinct geological areas. The Indo-Australian plate is forcing its way underneath the Pacific plate (subducting, in geological jargon). The slow-motion stresses this imposes cause tremendous strain on the adjoining areas and the Pacific plate is being steadily buckled. The result is the towering mountains of the Southern Alps. They culminate in the grandeur of Aoraki (Mount Cook). In 1991 Mount Cook lost 20m from its summit in a cataclysmic slide of ice and rock.

Geologists calculate that the Southern Alps are growing in height at the rate of 25mm a year. It is only the massive erosional effects of the heavy rainfall which keep the mountain heights reasonably static. The collapse on Mount Cook is an every day event when viewed from the geological perspective.

Forcing its way under the Pacific plate isn't all the Indo-Australian plate is doing. The two plates are sliding sideways as well. Areas such as the Red Hills of South Westland have geological matches in the Nelson area. Over time the two plates have moved about 480 km relative to each other. Geologists argue about the time frame in which this has occurred, with the figures ranging from 12 to 140 million years.

The presence of the Alpine fault gives life on the Coast a certain "edge". Current estimates suggest that there is a major earthquake on the Alpine fault every 500 years or so. We've now had around 500 years since the last big one. Like people on the San Andreas fault, we all know that one day the big one will come. In the meantime every small quake is greeted with a certain amount of enthusiasm, the reasoning being, probably fallacious, that this relieves stresses.

In recent times the Coast has still had some impressive quakes. The Murchison earthquake of 1929 (7.6 on the Richter scale) killed 17 people and uplifted a large area. More recently, the 1968 Inangahua Junction quake (7.1 on the Richter scale) killed three people. Such was the severity of the shock that numerous landslides occurred, one of which blocked the Buller River until the water behind the dam broke through. Scars from this jolt are still evident throughout the Buller Gorge. More recently, Westport suffered minor damage in 1991 from a quake which toppled chimneys and broke windows, although no-one was injured.

The landforms of the region are inextricably linked with the climate. The Southern Alps, built by the uplift of the plate interaction, directly affect the South Island's weather. Warm moist westerly air is forced upwards by the mountains and as it cools and condenses, rain falls. Higher still, the cooling results in snow. This extraction of moisture leaves the east coast relatively dry. Together, snow and rain have worked on the raw material provided by the battle of the plates. The end result is a series of spectacular glaciers, rivers, lakes and gorges.

The Coast is renowned for its rain, best summarised by the following poem which was written 50 years ago by a visitor to Hokitika:

It rained and rained and rained —
The average fall was well maintained.
And when the tracks were simply bogs,
It started raining cats and dogs.
After a drought of half an hour,
We had a most refreshing shower,

(Above) **Massive landslide in the Buller Gorge was triggered by the 1968 Inangahua Junction earthquake.**

(Above) **Early morning mist over the Grey River railway bridge at Greymouth.**

And then the most curious thing of all,
A gentle rain began to fall.
Next day also was fairly dry,
Save for a deluge from the sky,
Which wetted the party to the skin,
And after that — the rain set in.

There is little doubt that the Coast receives a generous and reliable rainfall. Many places vie for the unenviable title of the wettest place on earth and for parts of the Coast the assertion is as valid as any. Mount Waialeale on Kauai in Hawaii claims 12 metres a year but there are several places on the Coast where this figure has been exceeded. The Hydrological Survey of the then Ministry of Works and Development recorded mind-boggling figures from the Cropp. They registered annual rainfall figures of close to 14m on a number of occasions. During heavy rain in 1982, Franz Josef lost both its airstrip and its bridge. At Alex's Knob, 72 inches (1.83m) of rain was recorded within a 72 hour period, at which point the gauge overflowed and it was still raining.

Coasters will tell you, with some truth, that while the Coast is wet it is rarely unpleasant. For one thing, much of the rain occurs at night and when it falls in the daytime it is relatively warm. Hokitika, Westport and Haast boast nearly the same sunshine hours as Christchurch. Although much-maligned Greymouth has fewer sunshine hours than Christchurch, it beats Dunedin. Temperatures inland may become hot in summer and cold in winter, but in the coastal towns the range is small. Most Coasters neither swelter in summer nor freeze in winter.

The rivers on the Coast are for the most part short, steeply graded and flood-prone. The proximity of the ranges to the coast means a short response time to heavy rain events. Just a few hours of rain can cause rapid increases in flow rates. However, when flooding occurs it is usually short-lived. Greymouth had two massive floods within a few months in 1988. The damage was so severe that the town requested funding for and then built a flood wall. To date this has kept the river out of the town and raised the confidence of business folk.

Like most West Coast towns, Greymouth is built on a flood plain and estuary. Tales of previous events strain the imagination. In one flood, vessels tied up at the Greymouth wharf had to run their engines at full power to prevent being ripped from their moorings. Mind you, this may be due to bureaucracy rather than expediency. The engineering certificate for the Greymouth wharf still requires ships to be moored to a land-based deadman and run engines ahead when the river is in flood.

Another story, probably apocryphal but immortalised in song, tells of a Greymouth hotel's trip out to sea:

In Greymouth, in Greymouth, at the good old Rose and Thistle,
a bunch of thirsty miners came one night to whet their whistle.
Above the swish of wind and rain you could hear their glasses clink,
there was whisky, whisky everywhere and plenty of beer to drink.

In Greymouth, in Greymouth, the rain began to pour,
until the river rose in flood and reached the bar room floor.
The night wore on, the storm grew worse and they didn't sleep a wink.

(Above) **Nature's watercolours: the Ngakawau River by the Charming Creek Walkway suspension bridge.**
(Overleaf) **When it rains in South Westland it pours, but the moss helps regulate the flow.**

Near Karamea is the Honeycomb Cave complex, a treasury of subfossil remains containing more than 50 species. (Clockwise from Right) **Stalactites produce strange convolutions as they grow down from the cave roof; moa bones lay undisturbed for centuries; stalactite and stalagmite formations; the aptly-named elephant's feet.**

(Right top) **Sandstone detail on the Stockton plateau. The rich reds are presumably the result of iron deposits.** (Right lower) **Moss, lichen and algae-covered boulders beside a South Westland road.** (Overleaf) **The Oparara Arch, 200m long, 39m wide and 37m high, was scoured out over the millennia by the Oparara River.**

There was water, water everywhere and nothing to do but drink.

In Greymouth, in Greymouth, the building took a slide
and with its tipsy crew on board went walloping down the tide.
But where this crazy cruise would end not one of them could think
with water, water everywhere and far too much to drink.

In the north of the region water has produced some spectacular limestone formations amongst the karst landscape. Near Karamea, in the proposed new Kahurangi National Park, lies the Honeycomb Cave complex. This labyrinth, which was first surveyed between 1982 and 1984, continues to reveal new secrets to potholers.

Limestone features have their own dedicated vocabulary, bewildering to the beginner but immensely satisfying once you have learned a few terms. Water-worn limestone rock or limestone deposits such as stalactites and stalagmites are known as speleothems. Sinkholes, where underground systems have been intercepted by vertical tunnels, are a rich repository of recently extinct animals. In the Honeycomb Cave complex these include a giant native frog, several species of moa and many other birds, including the giant New Zealand eagle.

Further south in the Paparoa National Park, the power of water to shape a landscape is plain to see. The Park is traversed by rivers and creeks, each in its own canyon. Streams don't play fair in this region. They disappear into the ground only to resurface several kilometres away, often with no apparent regard for the surface topography.

Sandwiched between the two limestone areas are the Ngakawau and Buller

(Top) **Fox Glacier is advancing rapidly after heavy snow in recent years. South Westland's glaciers are unique in that they penetrate lush temperate rainforest.** (Lower) **Hire an experienced alpine guide to lead you onto Fox or Franz Josef Glacier. Steve Edwards of Alpine Guides cuts steps in the glacier with his icepick.** (Right) **Waterfalls abound in the steep valleys west of the main divide.**

Rivers. The Ngakawau, in the news for its hydroelectric potential, possesses one of the most spectacular gorges in New Zealand. Sadly perhaps, it is all but inaccessible. Helicopters are an easy but expensive way to enjoy this fascinating place. The Ngakawau can flood with unimaginable ferocity, especially in the gorge where the width is reduced. Rocks the size of houses lie strewn in the riverbed. Mere pebbles the size of cars are moved every time it floods.

The Buller River is much larger and longer than the Ngakawau, with its origins in the mountains behind Lake Rotoiti and Lake Rotoroa. The river has carved two spectacular gorges, named with great originality, the Upper and Lower gorges. These were first brought to European notice by the efforts of Thomas Brunner. In December 1846, Brunner set out from Nelson with two Maori guides and their wives to find the source of the Buller and follow it to the sea. Along the way the party ran out of food and Brunner was forced to eat his dog Rover.

After exploring as far south as Tititira Point at mouth of the Paringa River (marked by a monument at the southern end of the Paringa River bridge), the party wintered-over at the Arahura Pa and then sought a pass across the Southern Alps north of the Grey River. After 560 days of incredible hardship, Brunner (who had long been given up as dead) arrived back in Nelson. He survived only through the efforts of his Maori guides, Kehu and his wife. They remained loyal to him after the other couple, showing great commonsense, deserted the party.

While we believe Brunner's efforts were quite extraordinary, it must be remembered that his Maori companions not only went every step of the way with him but ensured his survival with their food-gathering skills. The journey ranks with any that Livingstone and other explorers of the era managed. Brunner eventually secured the post of Nelson's Commissioner of Public Works. He remained unimpressed by the West Coast, having failed to find areas fit for settlement or any glint of gold. However he did find coal and this set in train larger scale prospecting.

The heavy snowfalls on the Southern Alps during winter do much more than provide the east coast hydro lakes with water during the summer melt. They pile up in huge drifts and eventually compact into ice. As the snow continues to accumulate and compact, gravity takes over and a river of ice moves inexorably towards the sea.

These are best seen at the Franz Josef and Fox glaciers which, with the possible exception of some in South America, come closer to sea level than any other temperate region glaciers. Nowhere else in the world do glaciers penetrate into lush temperate rainforest.

The glaciers have long been enticing tourists. Even in the days when getting to the Coast was an adventure on the Cobb and Co. stagecoach, the glaciers were a prime tourist attraction. You can take the easy way out and view them from the comfort of the carpark but this is ultimately dissatisfying. For a modest fee you can be taken up onto either glacier by competent alpine guides.

During the last ice age both glaciers and others such as the Taramakau, Arahura and the Buller ran across the continental shelf and out to the sea. As the planet warmed the glaciers retreated. Since the last major retreat there has been a series of mini-advances and retreats. Currently, because of heavy snow over the last few years, both the Franz and Fox glaciers are advancing rapidly. A metre a day may not sound much but in geological terms this is a veritable sprint.

The névé region at the top of the glacier is an almost impenetrable jumble of twisted and fractured ice, run through at regular intervals by deep crevasses. It is not a place for people to venture onto without a guide. It is well worth visiting though and many take the easier option of flying, either by fixed wing or helicopter. The views from both are spectacular.

That glaciers are and were a potent force in shaping the landscape is immediately obvious coastwards of both the Fox and the Franz Josef. High U-shaped valleys run all the way to the coastal plain. Elsewhere in the South Island, most notably the southern lakes, the valleys have been occupied by water to form large, deep, steep-sided lakes.

There are lakes like this on the Coast. Lake Brunner, the region's largest and also one of its deepest, is of glacial origin. Like many of the streams which run through the native forest, the water is acidic and deeply stained. The colour, reminiscent of tea or beer (depending upon your inclination), is a result of tannins and humic acids in the water. Not all of the lakes or streams are this colour. Lake Kaniere near Hokitika, also glacially gouged, is clear. Some lakes such as Lake Christabel have formed as result of landslides, probably generated by large earthquakes.

While the Franz Josef and Fox glaciers receive most visitor attention because of their accessibility, there are others with equal claims for attention. Residents of Haast claim that the Landsborough Glacier far surpasses either of its northern cousins.

GOLD

(Top) **Thomas Phillips, a retired gold prospector.** (Lower) **The Kaniere water race where it crosses Bluebottle Creek. It was constructed to provide water and power for gold mining.** (Right) **Untreated alluvial gold at The Gold Room in Hokitika.**

DESPITE Brunner's jaundiced observation that "there is nothing on the West Coast worth incurring the expense of exploring", surveyors and gold prospectors continued to endure the hardships the terrain and climate imposed. The government of the day certainly had an eye for the main chance. In 1860 Assistant Native Secretary James Mackay purchased the bulk of the West Coast for 300 gold sovereigns. Mackay had been provided with 400 sovereigns for the purchase but saved 100 on the deal. It is unclear whether the signatories to this contract knew what they were signing away. Over the next 10 years, £12,000,000 worth of gold was to be taken from the Coast.

According to Leslie Hobbs in his book *The Wild West Coast*, a civil servant questioned the right of one Chief Tainui to claim ownership of the land he sold. According to the bureaucrat, the land belonged to someone else. Not true, said Tainui, he had eaten the person referred to. This, in Tainui's impeccable logic, transferred all land rights to himself. Tainui's claim was subsequently upheld. One hopes that this precedent is not well established in law.

Civil servants have not changed much over the years. Far from being delighted with Mackay's business acumen, they castigated him for the condition of the deed of sale. It mattered little that Mackay had been swept off his horse while crossing a river and had only just held onto his 100 sovereigns and the deed. He was advised to take greater care with important government documents in the future.

Although gold was found along the Buller River in 1859, there was little initial interest as the Otago gold rush was the main attraction for the itinerants who worked the fields. The West Coast gold rush got under way properly in 1865 as the Otago and Victorian goldfields began to peter out. At first the rewards were quite fabulous as the easy alluvial and beach deposit gold was worked out.

The lure of gold brought thousands to the Coast and helped shape the way in which the region would develop. Hokitika for instance had an official population of 4688 in 1867. This compares with 4000 today. The 1867 figure does not take into account the huge number of itinerants. In the two years to 1867, some 37,000 passengers disembarked at Hokitika, about one third of them Irish.

More gold passed through Hokitika last century than through any other town on the Coast. It was ill-equipped to cope. Many vessels were wrecked on the notorious Hokitika bar but people considered the risks reasonable. One party of four who worked the rich alluvial deposits of Okarito to the south of Hokitika sold 50 kg of gold. This was the result of three months' labour and worth around $900,000 at today's prices.

(Top) **Alluvial mining is an important contributor to the West Coast economy. In a typical operation a hydraulic excavator loads alluvium into a rotating screen, often on a floating unit. Large stones and rocks are rejected and gold particles settle on the riffle boards.** (Lower) **Leonie Finch-Batten, apprentice jeweller at The Gold Room, solders small nuggets onto a pendant.**

The rush, while it lasted, saw small towns sprout like mushrooms all over the Coast. Some such as Charleston still exist but at a fraction of their former population and glory. Others such as Goldsborough and Notown have completely disappeared.

At its peak, Hokitika boasted an opera house and a stock exchange. At one stage the town had 102 hotels or saloons to cater for the needs of miners. While there were dancing girls and saloon girls aplenty, historians have debated the level of prostitution. One argument held that the large proportion of Irish (and Catholic) miners made for a relatively moralistic society. It has also been suggested that because there were so few women they were "placed on a pedestal" and there was strong pressure for them to remain there.

Despite the number of grog shops, Hokitika was also known as a relatively sober town. Opinions vary as to why this should be so. One school of thought has it that the miners were so fit and healthy that they could handle their booze. A more likely explanation is that their alcohol was watered down by unscrupulous hotel owners.

Gambling was however part of the way of life. As always when there is easy money to be made, wagers were high. The Irish miners were good poker players and once took the notorious Bully Hayes to the cleaners. Bully arrived from the tropical Pacific and went ashore for a poker game. He went back to his boat practically bereft of shirt, an event considered so remarkable that it was reported in the local paper.

Alluvial gold comes from the weathering of gold-bearing ores. In 1870 Patrick Kelly, a prospector, found gold in the quartz deposits around Reefton. Soon there were over 50 quartz mines registered and the town became known, in the fashion of the day, as Quartzopolis. The claims stretched from Lyell in the north to Waiuta in the south. There seemed to be a particular pride in finding just the right name for the mine. Names range from the outright defiant to the hopeful, wistful or pragmatic. Examples include the Hopeful, Fiery Cross, Just-in-Time, Invincible, Perseverance, Golden Treasure, Keep-it-Dark, Wealth of Nations, and Energetic.

The stamping batteries they used worked on a simple principle. Heavy weights were dropped repeatedly onto gold-bearing quartz until it was fine enough for mercury or cyanide to dissolve any gold which was present. Gold was then removed from the cyanide by chemical means or the mercury heated until the gold was left behind. The crushing batteries required large amounts of energy. Many were powered by waterwheels while others relied on the plentiful supply

COURTESY WEST COAST HISTORICAL MUSEUM, HOKITIKA

of steam from burning cheap coal, readily available from the nearby coal mines. Surprisingly, none utilised electricity when it became available in 1886. It is commonly accepted that Reefton was the first town in the Southern Hemisphere to have electricity. Alas, Tamworth in Australia installed electric street lighting in 1885. Nonetheless Reefton was the first town south of the Equator to have a public electricity supply.

The quartz mines continued to produce well into the 20th century and one, the Blackwater mine at Waiuta, closed on 17 July 1951. Even then it did not close because it ran out of gold-bearing quartz. Eight days earlier "a disastrous cave-in occurred in the South Shaft, destroying the ventilation system and putting the pumping system out of action. In spite of all efforts to restore ventilation and get operating again the mine had to be abandoned." (Quoted in *The Golden Reefs* by D.J. Latham.)

At the time it closed, the Prohibition shaft was the deepest in New Zealand at 803m. Phoenix-like, the Prohibition may yet reopen. The New Zealand company MacRaes Mining plans to reopen the shaft and is considering full-scale production. Modern technology provides the means of pumping out the shaft and restoring the necessary ventilation.

Once the easy alluvial gold deposits were depleted, miners turned to other

(Left top) **Gold sluicing at Kumara, date unknown;** (Above) **Sluice boxes, circa 1930s;** (Left lower) **Dillmanstown in its heyday: a modern environmentalist's nightmare. Photographs like these are part of the rich legacy of the gold mining era which convey so graphically what life was like in the good old days. Visit a local museum or pub for a wider selection.**

methods. Sluicing was popular. High-powered water cannon were directed at suitable areas of gold-bearing sediment. The run-off, conducted through a series of "riffle boxes", dropped the heavier gold while carrying the lighter particles away. This gravity separation method was also the mainstay behind the giant gold dredges which were used on so many West Coast rivers.

There is a modern equivalent of these early juggernauts now operating on the Grey River at Ngahere. Originally designed with a cutter head as well as dredge buckets, it was considered unworkable by many locals. And so it proved. The company went into receivership and has recently been bought by a Coaster. Armed with local knowledge, he has refitted the giant 4000 tonne dredge and it is now back in operation, hopefully profitably.

The Coast is littered with gold claims. The methods used by the old-timers were not particularly efficient at recovering gold and it is worthwhile to dredge areas which have already been covered. With a hydraulic excavator, a modern alluvial miner can get deeper than the original prospectors and mine much more efficiently. In areas of waterlogged soil, mining with proper restoration can actually enhance agricultural productivity. Many a farmer on the West Coast has received both a royalty and increased yields from rehabilitated fields. There is a price to pay for alluvial mining. Unless extreme care is taken, fine sediment escapes into adjacent rivers and streams. Aesthetically this is unacceptable and impacts on many people. Although most West Coast miners play by the rules, there are a few mavericks out there who will cut corners in an attempt to make a buck.

The legacy of the old-timers is all around us. The remains of many crushing batteries are scattered around the Reefton area. One, the Snowy River battery which serviced the Blackwater mine, still retains its old cyanide tanks and various other rusted but still impressive items.

On the left hand side on the way into Kumara from Otira on State Highway 73 there are many impressive tailings. These are heaps made from large stones separated from the other material and deposited manually by industrious Chinese labourers. Some of the mounds are 10 to 15 metres high and give a good view of the surrounding piles. Be careful if you climb one of these as the rocks may move.

West Coast alluvial gold is amongst the purest in the world, being 96-98% pure in its natural form. Most of the gold is melted down into bars and exported but some is retained on the Coast. The Gold Room in Hokitika specialises in natural West Coast nuggets. These can be bought in their natural form or as jewellery. The precious metal still figures large in the West Coast economy. In 1991 around $30 million worth of gold was won.

You can try your own hand at gold panning. The recreated gold mining village of Shantytown just south of Greymouth will give you lessons and guarantee a trace of "colour" in your pan. If you get the taste for it there are several places under Department of Conservation control where you can try gold panning without a licence.

(Above) **You can try your hand panning for some "colour" at Shantytown pioneer village near Greymouth.**

COAL

"You're born here, you get used to it and you stay here.
I've been in coal mining all my life but now I've retired
we've thought about moving away but I don't think we ever will."

— Frank Hudson, retired coal miner, Reefton.

COAL was first discovered by Brunner during his epic West Coast trip at the site of what was to become the Brunner mine. As gold started to decline in importance, coal slowly replaced it. The largest of the early mines were at Denniston on the Denniston plateau just north of Westport and at Millerton on the Stockton plateau a little further north. At its peak, Denniston employed 250 men underground and the thriving township boasted a population of 2000.

The plateau is precipitous and presents a huge challenge to anyone trying to extract coal in bulk. The engineering solution arrived at was a steep incline over 1.7 km long. It was built in 1878-79 and became world-renowned as a marvel of technology. Even today when all but the slope have disappeared, it impresses. Each wagon was loaded at the top of the incline with eight tonnes of coal and then lowered on an endless steel cable system. Empty wagons were pulled back up the incline by the weight of the descending ones. Accidents were frequent and on several occasions the wire broke. Maximum slope on the incline was 47°.

The mine produced 12.6 million tonnes of coal during its 70 years of operation. The incline closed in 1967 after which the town went into decline. A recent census showed Denniston to have a population of 12. It's a wild and lonely existence on the plateau. The barren expanse of sedimentary rock is a harsh environment for plants and an even harsher one for humans. There are often weeks at a time when the plateau is wreathed in mist.

Worker attitudes towards the place were obviously rather jaundiced:

Damn Denniston
Damn the track
Damn the way both there and back
Damn the wind and damn the weather
God damn Denniston all together.

One man's view of Denniston from J.T. Ward's *Recollections of a Lifetime on the West Coast of the South Island.*

Further north, the Stockton plateau gives an indication of what Denniston must have been like when it was working. Here Coalcorp operates two large open cast mines. Coal is carried to the coastal railhead at the little township of Ngakawau by a 7.7 km long aerial ropeway at the rate of up to 250 tonnes per hour. Each of the 378 buckets on the line contains 1.4 tonnes of coal. On arrival at Ngakawau it is sorted and transferred into 49 tonne railway wagons. At present train loads of these wagons make the 400 km journey to the port of

(Above) **An open cast coal mine on the Stockton plateau. The excavator is dwarfed by the thickness of the coal seam.**

Lyttelton for export. The coal is much in demand overseas for its low ash and good coking properties.

Coalcorp is investigating the building of a jetty for loading bulk coal carriers off Westport. If this project goes ahead, the viability of the trans-Alpine railway line would be called into question to the detriment of many tourist establishments on the West Coast. In 1992 the Stockton-Webb mines sent 714,500 tonnes down the aerial ropeway. These two mines contributed the bulk of the record 1.2 million tonnes of coal worth $80 million which were extracted on the Coast during that year. This represented 40% of New Zealand's production and all of its bituminous coal. Further West Coast coal projects could boost this total quite considerably over the next few years.

It is possible to visit Stockton but intending visitors should contact the Coalcorp office in Westport first. Like the Denniston plateau, the even higher Stockton plateau (850m above sea level) is barren apart from pockets of growth in the valleys. There is little soil because the coarse marine sandstone bedrock contains few available nutrients. Even the streams provide little incentive for life. Deep within the coal seams, sulphuric acid forms from sulphides in the coal. The reaction is enhanced by the presence of specialised bacteria which use the sulphides as an energy source. The end result of this strange combination is highly acidic water. For those of a scientific bent it is noteworthy that streams on the Stockton plateau have been measured with pHs as low as 2.8. It is hardly surprising that such an environment is inimical to life.

(Top) **Miners at the end of their shift at the Strongman mine at Rapahoe.** (Middle) **Winding gear above the Denniston Incline. This is one of the few easily recognisable structures remaining after the mine closed in 1967.** (Lower) **The Ironbridge mine on the Denniston plateau still smokes many years after it was abandoned.**

Occasionally wisps or even columns of smoke can be seen issuing from cracks in the plateau. These are the result of fires in earlier underground mines and are almost impossible to put out. There are many old mine shafts up here, some from the Millerton mine but there are others.

Several kilometres up the Ngakawau River, Charming Creek joins the rush down the gorge. Charming Creek was once home to a thriving coal mine as well as a timber industry. The mine owners installed a narrow gauge railway line to carry coal the 10 km to Ngakawau. It was quite an engineering feat, apart from one glitch when two tunnelling crews, working from opposite ends, nearly missed each other, thereby causing a kink in the tunnel.

A Department of Conservation walking track now follows the course of the old railway line. Sadly the original bridge across the Ngakawau (itself a replacement) has been swept away but Fijian soldiers, in the area on an exercise, built a fabulous swingbridge in its place. The track has a great deal to offer including views of the 50m Mangatini Falls, spectacular forest and mountain views and

unusual flora and fauna. The track terminates some 12 km away from the old coal mining town of Seddonville. The walk is best appreciated by starting from the Seddonville end.

Coal measures are scattered through the Karamea, Buller, Reefton and Greymouth areas. Historically these have supported many mines, most of them underground. Underground mines used to be extremely labour intensive and many people on the Coast were supported directly or indirectly by the industry.

It was a hard and dangerous life. In 1896 there was an underground explosion at the Brunner mine site just up the Grey River from Greymouth. All 65 people underground at the time died in the tragedy. It remains New Zealand's worst mining disaster.

Tragically, 186 children were left fatherless, devastating the local community. The size of the funeral cortège, a kilometre long with 6000 people and six bands, indicates the trauma the deaths inflicted. Surprisingly perhaps, the mine reopened and was productive until 1906 before finally being abandoned in 1940. Fifty-eight victims of the disaster are buried in a mass grave in the Stillwater cemetery. The mine site has been preserved by the Department of Conservation and the brickworks and beehive coke ovens remain relatively intact.

More recently, in 1967, 19 men were killed in the Strongman underground mine at Rapahoe. Like the Brunner disaster, this was caused by an underground explosion. The original mine is soon to be closed and a new one opened further up the valley.

Up the Grey Valley, in the foothills of the Paparoa Range, is the settlement of Blackball. Originally founded on gold, coal soon supplanted it in importance. There is still an operating open cast coal mine at the head of the valley. Trucks from the Roa mine carry coal to a sorting and grading plant near the Blackball township.

In 1908 coal miners in Blackball struck, for a 30 minute instead of 15 minute lunch break. This led directly to the formation of the Federation of Miners and indirectly to the New Zealand Labour Party. For many years Blackball was a "hotbed" of Marxism. They were always a stroppy lot. In 1931-32 the miners struck for 15 months, at the time the longest strike in New Zealand's history. At times during the strike as many as 46 policemen were based in the town. The Blackball Hilton, once a hotel, now offering budget accommodation and no longer licensed, exhibits two of the strikers' banners. In 1947 the Blackball community started a workingman's club in protest at an increase of a penny a pint on beer in the local hotels (it went up from sixpence to sevenpence).

BOB McKERROW

(Top) **Old coal skips near the Millerton mine on the Stockton plateau.** (Lower) **Rusting relic of an abandoned coal mine.**

FORESTS & FORESTRY

"En route down the western side of the Divide... you skirt through one of the wonders of the living world; mixed podocarp beech forest growing cheek by jowl with living ice."

David Bellamy, botanist, in Moa's Ark, 1990.

(Above) **Two northern rata trees in the Oparara Basin near Karamea. They begin life in the tops of trees, send roots earthwards and eventually strangle the host.** (Right) **Paparoa National Park coastline is typified by steep cliffs and groves of nikau palm.**

FOR a variety of reasons the West Coast retained the bulk of New Zealand's remaining forests, a situation which is occasionally a cause for conflict. Initially trees were felled for local uses — to service the local communities, for water races associated with alluvial mining and for mine pit props.

As the rest of New Zealand converted its once vast tracts of forest into farmland, West Coast timber became more and more important until it became one of the region's major export industries. The situation hasn't changed much. Current estimates place the value of forestry and timber production on the Coast at $35-40 million annually.

The battle for control of West Coast timber was bitter and long. Conservationists objected to clear felling which was devastating areas of outstanding natural and scientific beauty. These people saw the same thing happening on the Coast which had already occurred in the rest of the country and they wanted it stopped. After much acrimony The West Coast Accord was signed. This set the scene for the establishment of the Paparoa National Park and the transfer of much productive forest into the conservation estate. In return, conservationists agreed to allow continued clear felling of some native forests until exotic plantation timber was sufficiently mature to replace it. Other areas were to be managed on a sustainable yield basis only. These moves were to ensure the continued viability of mills and the communities they supported.

Unfortunately, the Government did not entirely keep its side of the bargain and the exotics (mostly Tasmanian blackwoods and radiata pine) required to keep the South Westland communities viable were not planted soon enough nor in sufficient numbers. To compensate for adding another 311,000 hectares of forest to the conservation estate, the Government made a substantial cash contribution to the South Westland community. This was spent in a number of ways including an attractive visitor centre at Haast. The Department of Conservation and its local advisory group partners used treated pine for the building after outrage over the planned use of the cheaper native rimu, then being milled on a non-sustainable basis.

Although there is still a group of disgruntled Coasters who feel that everything on the Coast is being "locked up", those who have taken the new opportunities offered are well satisfied. Over-enthusiastic projections of visitor arrivals did not help the conservation cause either, but tourism now ranks with farming as the West Coast's main revenue earner. All the indications are that it will continue to increase.

Native timber, mostly rimu, is still being extracted on a non-sustainable basis

SPHAGNUM

A BUSINESS THAT'S PICKING UP

(Above) **Only longer strands of good colour fetch the higher prices.** (Right) **Sphagnum moss pickers loading bales.**

MENTION the word moss to most people and they will automatically think of small green low-lying plants that look… well… mossy. True mosses belong to a group of very primitive green plants which have no proper root system, no transport vessels for moving sap around the plant and do not produce flowers.

Their life-cycle is unusual by human standards. After fertilisation has taken place the adult plant produces a tall thin sprout. This sprout, technically a sporophyte, grows almost parasitically on the adult. When it is mature it produces spore capsules which release thousands of spores. The spores lucky enough to find a secure damp spot, germinate to form the gametophyte and the cycle begins again.

So much for the biology lesson. Sphagnum moss is a major industry on the Coast and is viable and sustainable. Until the early 1980s, sphagnum moss was considered merely part of the countryside. It grows in poorly-drained pakihi soils which in most other places would be called bogs (on the Coast nearly all land is boggy). By moss standards, New Zealand sphagnum is a giant with strands frequently growing to 25cm or more and it is this length that gives it its overseas appeal.

The industry supports 400 workers locally and has grown rapidly over the years. The reasons for this are varied. The West Coast Regional Development Council quickly grasped the potential of this unusual crop and carried out both market and product research. The result of this input, coupled with a willingness to learn on behalf of both pickers and exporters, is the world's best sphagnum moss product.

Orchid growing is a huge and very profitable industry in Japan. However it is an arcane "science". Propagation from seed is difficult, time-consuming and hence expensive. Orchid seeds require the presence of special commensal fungi before they'll germinate. Modern cell culture techniques provide a way around all this. Any fancied orchid variety can be propagated from just a few cells by placing them in the correct nutrient medium and allowing them to grow. When each of these tiny plants is big enough it can be divided up again and the process allowed to repeat. With time, thousands, if not millions, of genetically identical orchids can be reared.

When the cloned orchids are large enough to be separated from their nutrient agar jelly, their root ball is carefully wrapped in wet sphagnum and they are potted. After approximately six months of growth they are transferred to a larger pot and a new wrapping of sphagnum. Why sphagnum? Why not some high-tech plastic substitute?

Sphagnum has a variety of attributes that make it perfect for potting

orchids. It will hold up to 20 times its own weight of water, so water retention is not a problem. Secondly, the plant itself alters the chemistry of the added water so that it becomes more acidic, a necessity with the most popular Japanese orchids. Finally, it is a relatively sterile medium which is essential in the hothouse conditions in which the orchids are reared.

A number of steps are required to produce export quality moss. The most important is to find a source. Although there are moss beds on private land, the bulk of the bogs occur on Department of Conservation, Landcorp or Timberlands property. The Timberlands resource is effectively locked up as they have entered into a commercial agreement with a major moss exporter. It is therefore the Department of Conservation and Landcorp areas which are sought after. At present the pickers tender for a 12-month licence to a particular area. They pay royalties, around $70 per wet tonne. Picking is an art: only longer strands with good green colour fetch the high prices. Short, broken or discoloured strands are left behind. It is these "outcasts" that provide the nucleus for the next crop 18 months to four years later.

Picked moss is placed in nylon carry sacks, which weigh around 100 kg each when full. As these are far too heavy to carry out, mechanical aids are required. In the early days people just took in trail bikes or four wheel drive vehicles. This was a mistake. The bogs are a very fragile environment and cannot withstand such pressures. Now the large exporters use helicopters.

The hobby pickers still do it the hard way. Most of them lack the drying facilities to handle large amounts of wet moss so have no need to carry out huge loads. Purists claim that the best moss is air-dried on racks but most of the large processers use drying kilns. Typically it is dried overnight at 40-50°C. Too much drying causes it to become brittle and lose colour, not enough and it fetches a lower price and is expensive to export. Around 120 kg of dry moss can be obtained from one-and-a-half wet tonnes. When dry it is removed from the kiln and sorted over screens. Matted pieces and short strands are removed at this stage. Finally it is packaged for export.

The price depends upon the quality, but good moss fetches around $13-15 per kilogram landed in Japan. The market may have reached its ceiling at around 500 tonnes. Limited amounts of moss go to Taiwan and the United States and perhaps this market may increase in the future.

There are competitors. Moss is harvested in Tasmania, North America, Chile and China but by some quirk of luck the quality and length does not compare with the New Zealand product. As long as commonsense prevails and picking is kept within sustainable levels, the West Coast will provide the world with this quality product in perpetuity.

(Above) **Processing the moss for export is an exacting task. West Coast sphagnum is the world's market leader due to its quality and length.**

in South Westland, under The West Coast Accord. Clear felling in the Okarito and Saltwater forests ceased some years ago and a new sustainable yield regime has been introduced.

This is innovative stuff. It is the first time that anyone has tried to manage, on a commercial sustainable yield basis, trees which take 500 years to mature. Extraction techniques are all-important. Traditional methods using forestry roads and haulers are too destructive so Timberlands West Coast Limited, the state-owned enterprise charged with managing the Government's timber reserves, has successfully used helicopter logging.

The contractors used a Russian heavy-lift helicopter which was capable of removing three tonnes of logs at a time. Depending upon the efficiency of the ground crews, the chopper was able to shift 100 tonnes of logs an hour. Tragedy struck in October 1993 when the helicopter crashed (not while it was logging), killing all three aboard. However, helicopters are ideal for this kind of logging and there is little doubt that this will be the method of the future.

There are few private forests on the West Coast. In mid-1993 the Government introduced brave legislation which prevented landowners from logging their native trees, except on a sustainable yield basis. So slowly do the trees grow, that for many this basically meant one tree could be extracted every year or so. While the Government has exempted itself from paying compensation to those who have been unable to realise their assets, they have also left huge gaps in the legislation. It is illegal to fell trees for furniture or building on a non-sustainable basis but perfectly legal to do so for firewood or to develop farmland. The law, as they say, is an ass.

A gross generalisation divides West Coast forests into three types. There are the various exotic plantations, mostly of *Pinus radiata*, an introduced conifer. Few have any objections to these plantations. Early settlers were enthusiastic in their clearance of lowland forest and in many situations the soil was of extremely low productivity. By planting with pine, otherwise unproductive land can provide a cash return. Pines have even been planted on old dredge tailings. They grow quickly and provide some vegetative cover on an otherwise austere scene.

When the discussion turns to native timber the conflicts begin. The forests of South Westland which are still being clear felled consist mainly of podocarps. These are conifers which have survived essentially unchanged since the days of the dinosaurs. Rimu is possibly the best known and is widely utilised as a timber. Kahikatea or white pine, New Zealand's tallest tree, is of limited practical use as the timber has no resin and hence has poor durability. It retains some specialist uses such as in marine quality plywood. Occasionally it is used as firewood but it is rarely felled these days. Other podocarps include miro, matai, several species of totara and some celery pines.

The name podocarp means "foot-fruit" and comes from the unusual arrangement of the seed. A fleshy, highly nutritious fruit hangs below the true seed. These are eagerly sought after by native birds during the fruiting season and are a major dietary item for many.

The new sustained yield management techniques and the phasing out of clear felling in South Westland should remove most conservationist concerns about utilising native podocarp forest.

The third type of forest is beech. If you enter the West Coast through any of the major passes this will be the forest you see. Three species make up the bulk

(Above) **Kahikatea trees in a lowland swamp in South Westland. New Zealand's tallest tree, the kahikatea sometimes reaches 60m. (Overleaf) Beech forest growing beside the Oparara River achieves naturally what the Japanese spend years trying to create in their wonderful gardens.**

of the trees: silver beech, hard beech and red beech. The wood is hard and durable but rarely utilised for timber except historically by some coal miners. Apparently supports made of beech will emit noise when under stress, giving the miner ample warning to effect modifications.

The problem with harvesting beech forest is that much of the timber is of poor quality. To harvest beech sustainably requires the clear felling of substantial patches (coupes) and managing the regrowth for higher quality timber. A high proportion of the trees felled in the original clearing has traditionally been chipped as the timber is of little use for anything else.

Despite the fact that a substantial area has been set aside for a West Coast beech scheme in The West Coast Accord, conservationists still oppose the concept. Beech regenerates rapidly and can reach a harvestable size in 50 years. The problem stems from the need to have 50 (or more) coupes in various stages of regeneration. During the growth phase the area available for native birds and other animals is reduced. This is the major cause for concern. Yet the reduction in available habitat, when taken on a regional basis, is minimal. Commonsense has gone out the window on this one and many conservationists talk emotive nonsense about the number of birds which will be deprived of a home. Undoubtedly some birds would die but the trade-off has already been made in the Accord. The size of the conservation estate is now sufficient that such loss should be tolerated. The basis for conservationist arguments stems from the concept of sustainability. This argument suggests that the total ecosystem must be sustainable, not just the trees.

So far the question seems relatively academic anyway. There is no sustained yield beech scheme on the West Coast and there appears to be little demand for the hardwood timber. This is a chicken and egg situation. If public awareness of the durability and quality of the wood were greater, then demand would certainly be higher. In a way it is a pity that the market has not been established. Sustainably grown beech timber may be able to replace some of the tropical rainforest timber which continues to be felled at an alarming rate. To date, the discussion has centred on commercial timber species but the West Coast forests are much more complex than this brief introduction suggests. Beech forests basically stop at the Taramakau River and don't start again until the Mahitahi River which lies just north of the Paringa River. This "beech gap" is believed to be a consequence of the last ice age when most of the area was swept clean by the ice of the numerous glaciers. Beech disperses slowly and has not yet managed to penetrate deeply into the gap.

More widely distributed are non-beech hardwoods which include two species of rata and many others such as kamahi. The northern rata starts life high in a tree, deposited there as a seed in a bird dropping. At first it grows as an epiphyte but with time produces aerial roots. These ultimately encircle the host and bite deeply into the bark, eventually strangling the host and depriving it of its sap supply. This may take 200 years or more but the end result is a rata tree growing around the rotting trunk of its host.

Southern rata lead a more sedate lifestyle and grow like most other self-respecting trees. Both species boast a brilliant display of crimson flowers which they produce in summer. Around the Otira Gorge these southern rata blossoms are particularly spectacular. In recent years the show all but disappeared. The Australian brush tailed possum, introduced to establish a fur industry in the

(Top) **A treefern on the banks of the Ngakawau River north of Westport. Take your camera with you wherever you go on the Coast.** (Lower) **Frosted fern leaves on the roadside near Blackball.** (Right) **Early morning mist, Lake Kaniere.**

(Top) **Southern rata in flower above Otira. Possum control operations by the Department of Conservation have restored the splendour after earlier depredations.** (Lower) **Native clematis flowers are an indication to Coasters that spring has arrived. These climbers festoon trees with their yellow and white flowers in late September through to November.** (Right top) **The forest is maintained by recycling. The stark veins of this dead leaf indicate that decomposers have already been at work.** (Right lower) **The forest floor is often carpeted by ferns. These umbrella ferns provide the subtle variations in colour that are so characteristic of South Westland rainforest.**

country, just loves rata leaves. Faced with massive selective browsing of new growth, trees were becoming stunted or dying.

Fortunately both the Regional Council and the Department of Conservation wage an unceasing war on possums, although for different reasons. Possums are carriers of bovine tuberculosis and when they feed on farmland may transmit the disease to cattle or deer. This has the potential to cripple the dairy industry. Also because possums selectively browse desirable native tree species to the almost total exclusion of others, they have been changing the structure of our native forests.

Possums are either trapped, poisoned or shot. In particularly rugged country the animal may be controlled by aerial drops of poisoned baits. The technique has been well established in this country. Carrot baits are prepared. These are first dyed green to reduce their attractiveness to birds and then have cinnamon added to appeal to the possums. Finally 1080 (monofluoroacetate), a nerve poison, is added and the carrot pieces are precision-dropped from either a helicopter or a topdressing aircraft. The results of possum control in the Otira region have been spectacular. Once again whole hillsides turn red with rata blossom in summer.

Deer used to be a problem too. These animals browse the understorey to the extent that young seedlings die and regrowth does not occur. During the 1970s helicopters carrying deer cullers were utilised to kill deer. As the price of venison went up the pressure on deer mounted and proved a very effective control. Deer farming also became popular and helicopters were used to net live deer. The pressure on the forests has been reduced and many West Coast farmers have diversified into deer farming.

But back to the vegetation. Characteristic of the West Coast is a profusion of ferns ranging from the giant tree ferns to tiny wisps. Nowhere else in the world do ferns make such a massive contribution to the flora. Together with the podocarps and beech they give a vivid reminder of what the rest of the world was like in a bygone era. This is one of the reasons for the recognition of the South West New Zealand World Heritage Area, Te Wahipounamu.

Nikau palms, New Zealand's only native palm, make their most southerly appearance on the West Coast. Again the Taramakau River seems to be the major boundary although a few stragglers may reach as far south as Poerua. Groves of nikau palms occur near Punakaiki and also at the start of the Heaphy Track near Karamea. Nikau are the most southerly palms in the world.

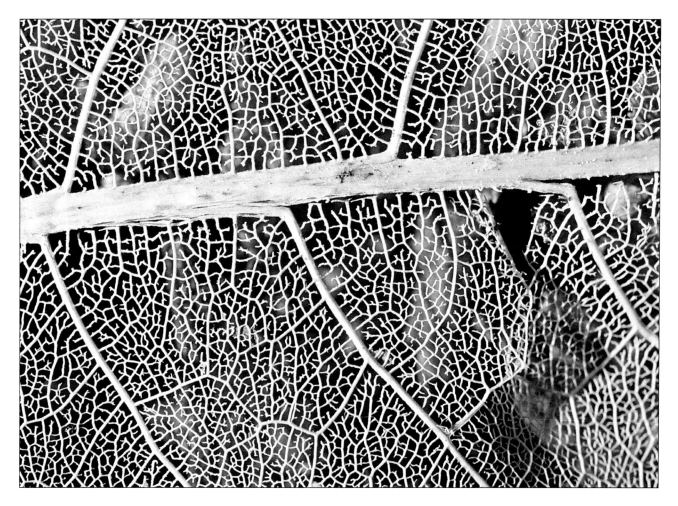

THE ANIMALS

(Above) **Beef and dairy farming is the West Coast's largest industry, although tourism is rapidly catching up.** (Right) **Kea, clowns of the mountains, may well be threatened despite their apparent abundance. If you leave your car unattended in kea country expect to find some minor damage on your return.**

MOST visitors to the West Coast will already be aware of some of the creatures they are likely to encounter. In fact animals such as seals and penguins are often the reason for the visit. However there is also a fascinating invertebrate fauna which is worthy of investigation.

Some of these are restricted to the karst landscapes referred to earlier. In fact the Honeycomb Cave complex near Karamea boasts two interesting and somewhat alarming beasties. One of these is a spider, *Spelungula*, New Zealand's biggest and most primitive. With a leg span of up to 15cm, this animal is not for the faint-hearted. *Spelungula* lives on the walls of caves and feeds upon insects which live in, or blunder into, the cave. Cave wetas are their major prey item. Wetas are large ground crickets and cave wetas are the most attenuated of the tribe with long legs and even longer antennae. They are found in most old mining tunnels and almost all caves. Cave wetas are easy to locate; just shine your torch on the roof of your cave. But watch out: they react to light by dropping off the roof, often straight into your upturned face.

Also found in limestone landscapes, but not restricted to the Karamea area, are the giant *Powelliphanta* snails. Like the spiders and wetas these are fully protected; it is even illegal to take their empty shells. *Powelliphanta* are voracious carnivores, hunting down and catching giant native earthworms many times longer than themselves.

You may not make the acquaintance of *Powelliphanta*, but it is absolutely certain that you will meet Te Namu, the sandfly. Sandflies, also known as blackflies, are the curse of the Coast. They belong to a group of biting flies called the Simuliidae. Females lay their eggs in fast flowing streams. When the larva hatches it spins itself, on a suitable stone, a silken pad to which it attaches by means of small hooks. It feeds by straining food particles out of the water. It then pupates and approximately seven weeks after the egg was laid, the adult rides a bubble of air to the surface where it pops out. After the wings harden it flies away. Only females suck blood. The male feeds on sap. A chemical in the saliva of the sandfly prevents blood from coagulating and it is this which causes stinging and swelling. They are very inefficient at escape so most sandflies which feed on humans die from a slapping hand. Yet they are very efficient at biting. Sandfly repellent works, although some Coasters claim that it attracts flies. In the early mining days miners used to smear themselves with bacon fat. Some claimed that this was worse than the sandflies.

Freshwater fish don't usually capture the imagination but on the West Coast they are an integral part of Coast folklore. A number of freshwater native fish

(Top) **The giant kokopu is the world's largest galaxiid fish. The juveniles make up around five percent of the whitebait runs on the West Coast.** (Middle) **Fisherman with brown trout, Rough River.** (Lower) **New Zealand scaup frequent clear water lakes where they can see food which they find during short dives. Male birds have a bright yellow eye.**

species, known as galaxiids, spawn in fresh or brackish water. When the eggs hatch the young go to sea to feed. Once they reach sufficient size, large schools of these tiny transparent juveniles ascend the rivers. These young fish, known as whitebait, are a delicacy of the highest order. They are usually cooked in patties. The taste is subtle, perhaps disappointing to smokers or those who possess an insensitive palate. The best whitebait patties are held together with just the yolk of an egg and a trace of salt and pepper for seasoning. If the catch is meagre, flour may be added to eke out the supply. Whitebait are not for everyone. There are a few who find the accusatory stare of hundreds of tiny glazed-over eyes too much to take.

The legal fishing season on the West Coast runs from 1 September to 14 November. It's a bad time for employers. Any sick leave which remains outstanding becomes mysteriously used up during the whitebaiting season and there are rashes of dead grandmothers. It is more of an obsession than a pastime and every fishable river hosts a throng of hopeful whitebaiters.

Fishing is with a scoop net or trap and on gazetted rivers people build small piers (known as stands or trenches) to contain their legal entitlement of trap nets. Until stands were licensed there were unseemly tussles over the best spots.

At the start of the season, whitebait usually fetches $40-50 per kilogram but as it progresses prices come down, particularly if there has been a good run. All baiters are liars. If they've been getting good catches they'll deny it; if they haven't caught a skerrick they'll tell you they are doing alright.

In the old days when there was no form of preservation except smoking or drying, excess whitebait were fed to chickens or used to fertilise the garden. These days excess catch is frozen and it is nearly always possible, at a price, to obtain some in New Zealand. Traditionally the biggest runs come from the Cascade River in the deep south of South Westland. The commercial whitebaiters here use light aircraft to fly their catches out to markets elsewhere in the country.

Whitebait provide the excuse for a whitebait festival in Westport. Amongst the more traditional activities usually seen at such times is one which is peculiarly West Coast. Contestants indulge in a whitebait filleting competition, using razor blades to strip pathetic little pieces of flesh from their tiny fish. On occasion showoffs attempt to use chainsaws.

Whitebait may even be responsible for the presence of the West Coast's best-known literary figure Keri Hulme, whose book *the bone people* won the Booker Prize in 1985. Keri lives in the tiny coastal settlement of Okarito and is an avid whitebaiter. She's even written a novel entitled *Bait* which chronicles the lives

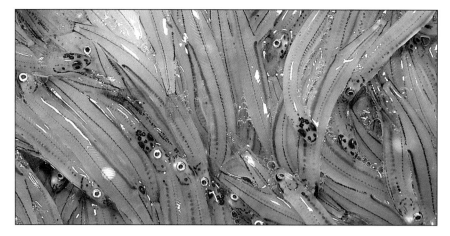

of a community suspiciously like the one in which she lives at Okarito.

The vertebrate fauna on land is more diverse than that found on West Coast streams. Amongst the remains found in the various cave complexes in the region are those of a giant recently extinct frog. Giant is a relative term but it was certainly much bigger than any of the three surviving native species, none of which is found in the South Island. If you find a frog it is likely to be the introduced Australian whistling frog. In 1875 a Mr W. Perkins brought some specimens from Tasmania in a bottle and liberated them in a drain in Alexandra Street, Greymouth. From there they spread to the Grey River and dispersed along the south bank for a number of kilometres. This casual and somewhat cavalier introduction proved successful from the frog's point of view as it has now spread widely through the Coast from sea level to mountain top. Its plaintive whistling is now the most characteristic sound of the West Coast bush.

Birds are usually immediately obvious to the visitor and there is plenty of choice as the West Coast boasts over 75 species, one of which is found nowhere else. There is insufficient space to do more than describe a small number of species. The interested reader is referred to the Suggested Reading list for further sources of information.

The bird most closely identified with the West Coast is the white heron or kotuku (see sidebar). Worldwide this is a common and widespread species but for reasons which are not yet understood it does not seem to be spreading within New Zealand. This is not true of the royal spoonbill, a bird which shares the white heron's nesting site. In recent years royal spoonbills have been ranging further and further away from the Coast and there are now several other nesting colonies elsewhere in the country.

Kereru, the native wood pigeons, are common. Their noisy laboured flight can even be heard in the towns. They are a surprisingly colourful bird and it is well worth taking the time to look at them through binoculars. During the nikau palm fruiting season they are easily spotted from the coastal walking tracks.

Tui and bellbirds can be found in most gardens. Tui are particularly fond of kowhai flowers and every tree has frequent visitors while the flowers last.

Kea soon make their presence felt. There is a resident gang of juveniles which moves between the Otira and Arthur's Pass tips, terrorising everything in between. At the Franz Josef and Fox glaciers kea really make their presence known. Unattended cars can be quite badly damaged as the birds rip off windscreen rubber, windscreen wiper rubbers or make holes in soft tops. Even

(Top left) **Freshly-caught whitebait, the West Coast's most famous delicacy.**
(Top right) **Whitebait patties, a subtle taste not appreciated by everyone.** (Lower) **A solitary whitebaiter inspects his catch.**
(Overleaf) **Spotted shags nesting at Perpendicular Point near Punakaiki. This colony is heavily populated because it is so secure from predators.**

THE KOTUKU

AN AVIAN NARCISSUS

(Above) **The kotuku can sometimes be spotted on the river's edge or shoreline. Despite its regal appearance, it is a rowdy bird.**

THE white heron bewitches both Maori and pakeha. The Maori called it kotuku. In the North Island, where it may have been encountered only once in a lifetime, it became a symbol of rarity. *He kotuku rerenga tahi*:"A white heron of a single flight". An honoured visitor could have his visit compared with that of the white heron. His importance became a reflection of the scarcity of the bird.

But Maori did not cherish the kotuku for its rarity alone. The nuptial plumes, long lace-like feathers grown during the breeding season, were a treasure almost beyond price. Caged herons were plucked at intervals. The plumes went to adorn the heads of chieftains. Each kind of plume had a name of its own. The longest, and hence the most highly valued, were only for the men; women were forbidden to wear them.

In general the kotuku was associated with manhood, as were most white things in the Maori world. A dream of skulls of ancestors adorned with plumes indicated the birth of a son was nigh, while dark huia feathers signalled that a daughter was imminent. The patience of a hunting heron did not escape the Maori either. Another proverb is hauntingly evocative. *He kotuku kai whakaata*, "a white heron, that feeds upon its reflection". The beauty of its reflection more than compensated it for the long wait for food. A sort of avian narcissus.

Historically the kotuku has never been common. Breeding has been restricted to a patch of stately kahikatea (white pine) forest on the banks of the Waitangiroto River, near Okarito in South Westland. Although the Maori prized the nuptial plumes of the kotuku, they did not exploit it to any great extent. Perhaps they never discovered the breeding site.

In the 1870s the Europeans discovered the Waitangiroto colony and this was nearly the end of it. Women's hats required feathers; white heron feathers were rare so this increased the snob value for anyone "lucky" enough to have one on display. In 1871 there were 25 nests; in 1877 there were only six. Fortunately fashions changed, in time to save the ostrich and white heron alike. The stately kotuku became forgotten.

In 1940 the colony was down to four nests, a precarious situation and one from which most species would never recover. But this near-disaster signalled the start of a conservation campaign that was to prove a triumph. Today there are around 150 white heron in New Zealand. Each spring they unerringly find their way back to the Waitangiroto River to breed.

Up until 1987, if you wanted to see the heron colony you had to obtain a permit and travel 6 km on foot through mud and swamp to the site. Now with a fresh outlook on conservation this has all changed. The Department

(Above) **Kotuku or white heron are synonymous with the West Coast despite their abundance elsewhere in the world. Many Coasters consider them Australian pests.**

of Conservation has built a large, sturdy, well-positioned hide. Across the river from the nests, it provides an excellent view of the white herons, shags and royal spoonbill that share the site.

To reach the hide a boardwalk has been built some distance upriver from the heron colony. White Heron Sanctuary Tours provide the access. Ken, Milan and Peter Arnold run jetboat tours from Whataroa or Franz Josef.

The boardwalk provides a fascinating view of New Zealand's equivalent of the Everglades. It is hard to believe that civilisation is so close in this primaeval environment. The colony has been aptly described by observers as "big blobs of cotton wool scattered amongst the vegetation".

The white herons build large untidy nests in low trees and make uneasy neighbours. If they are having trouble building their nest they will filch sticks from an unattended one. If the male leaves his lady alone, one of the bachelor males will sneak in for an attempted seduction. The noises from the colony belie the beauty of the birds.

Most Coasters feel quite ambivalent about kotuku. They appreciate their beauty but view them as sort of avian rats because of their propensity to scrounge food. With time an uneasy truce may evolve.

(Top) **Kaka are widespread on the West Coast but are rarely seen. They require old trees for nesting holes and are very vulnerable to habitat disturbance.** (Lower) **The smallest penguin is the little blue, which can occasionally be seen on beaches or crossing the road around coastal bluffs near Punakaiki and Karamea.**

in the high country nothing is safe. If you had figured on sleeping in some mornings you may well get a rude awakening as kea slide down the corrugated iron roofs of huts. They appear to do it for fun, for the same reason that they worry at the nails holding the roof on. A botanist working on plant distributions on an alpine transect had to allow for having a number of his marker pegs stolen by kea. If you leave breakable gear unattended, a quizzical kea is almost certain to "sample" it.

Kea appear numerous because of their apparent interest in human company. While they are not particularly endangered they could become so. The Department of Conservation discourages people from feeding the birds because they fill up on junk food and may become dependent on these human hand-outs.

The closely related kaka are not so frequently seen. Small flocks of them can be observed in almost any part of the Coast. They require big old trees for nesting holes and as these are removed, breeding success is reduced. They also require the honeydew produced by a bug which feeds on the sap of beech trees. Unfortunately, introduced German and common wasps also have a penchant for the dew. Wasp densities in some parts of the forest actually outweigh that of all the birds combined. Bereft of this high energy food, the kaka may suffer. Life is becoming increasingly difficult for these forest clowns.

Life is much rosier for the weka or native woodhen. Weka populations seem to ebb and flow to some as yet indeterminate cause. They appear to be on an upswing at present and are slowly increasing their populations. These wary birds are nearly as inquisitive as kea but much more subtle in their approach. If you camp near the bush and lose a teaspoon it has probably been stolen by a weka.

The commonest large bird is the pukeko or swamphen. These handsome birds thrive in the damp conditions which prevail on most of the Coast. Sometimes they achieve such high densities that local farmers will organise a "puke" hunt. Pukeko can be legally hunted and are occasionally eaten. One recipe calls for boiling the bird with a brick then throwing out the pukeko and eating the brick. If you want to sample the culinary delights to which pukeko can be put, visit the Hokitika Wild Foods Festival held every March.

Kiwi are still relatively common on the West Coast and often occur in the most unexpected situations. Evidence of their feeding forays can often be seen well above the treeline around alpine tarns. They are also much more catholic in their food tastes than was earlier believed. While they forage in leaf litter for worms and other invertebrates, they will also wade in shallow creeks and snaffle freshwater crayfish (koura).

Until recently, it was believed that there were three kiwis here, the South Island brown, the nearly extinct little spotted and the less threatened great spotted kiwi. It is now almost certain that the great spotted kiwi found around Okarito is a new species. Watch this space in future editions.

Amongst the predators, the harrier hawk is extremely common and reaches great densities for such a large bird. This is hardly surprising. Every morning there is a huge selection of dead possums to choose for breakfast. The carnage amongst possums must be dreadful but it helps keep the harriers fed and the forests safe. When you are driving, don't go out of your way to avoid a possum; it isn't worth an accident and will feed some needy hawk.

A truly fortunate visitor will see or hear a New Zealand falcon. These superbly streamlined birds are relatively rare but can be recognised by their speed of flight and their harsh "kek-kek-kek" cry.

At night the forest is taken over by the native owl, known as the morepork. The Maori name ruru is also very onomatopoeic. Morepork feed on anything they can catch from insects right through to other birds. They are occasionally encountered in daylight, usually hunkered down on a dark branch.

None of the birds mentioned to date belongs specifically to the West Coast. That honour goes to the Westland black petrel. The story of its discovery is typical of the Coast. Barrytown schoolchildren were doing a school project on what they thought was the sooty shearwater when they listened to a radio talk on the bird by Sir Robert Falla, renowned ornithologist and Director of the Dominion Museum in Wellington. They were somewhat puzzled by the statement that the sooty shearwater usually laid eggs around the end of November. Their bird laid around May. Confused by this six-month anomaly, they wrote to the great man who duly visited the colony and in 1946 described the Westland black petrel as a new species.

Thanks to the efforts of Bruce Stuart-Menteath and Denise Howard of Paparoa Nature Tours, you can visit the colony. You have a choice between dusk, when the birds return home for the night, or at dawn when they leave. The dawn departures are probably the most spectacular if you can manage the early start. Streams of the 1.25m wingspan birds clamber clumsily through the bush before launching into dives towards the nearby valley. Most pick up enough speed to clear the trees but every now and again one makes an undignified crash-landing and has to start again.

The adults are large and aggressive, quite capable of taking care of intruding rats or stoats. Unattended chicks are at risk during the day but Bruce operates a number of stoat, cat, and dog traps to reduce predation pressure. Over the past 20 years the population has doubled but has now peaked. Some ornithologists put this down to the increased availability of fish scraps from the large number of vessels which now fish the West Coast. Fifty percent of chick diet consists of fish offal.

Because of the relative rarity of several of New Zealand's penguin species, public awareness of these birds has increased enormously. These days everyone wants to see a penguin. If you visit South Westland during the breeding season from July to late November you will almost certainly be able to see a Fiordland crested penguin, the tawaki, arguably the world's rarest (although no-one yet knows for certain). There are easily accessible colonies at Monro Beach near the Lake Moeraki Wilderness Lodge and at Cascade Head near Jackson Bay. If you stay at the Wilderness Lodge, their enthusiastic guides will escort you to the colony.

Widely distributed along the length of the coast is the little blue penguin. These, the smallest of penguins, can sometimes be seen crossing coastal roads, often at altitudes of 100m or more. Size for size they must be the noisiest birds of all, as they are capable of producing the most bloodcurdling shrieks and moans.

Apart from introduced species, terrestrial mammals are restricted to two species of bat, one of which is found nowhere else. If you are extremely fortunate you will see one of these in South Westland but the chances are remote.

(Top) **The New Zealand falcon is a sleek efficient predator which is usually heard before it is seen.** (Lower) **Morepork or ruru can occasionally be encountered during the day while they rest on suitable branches. At night their mournful cry fills the bush.**

(Top) **Young Fiordland crested penguins become fully fledged and ready to leave the nest towards the end of November.** (Lower) **A group of Fiordland crested penguins waddle ashore at Monro Beach in South Westland.** (Right top) **An immature elephant seal resting on the beach at Arnott Point in South Westland. He is probably a straggler from the sub-Antarctic islands. Elephant seals feed on squid and fish which they catch on dives lasting up to half an hour.** (Right lower) **The Westland black petrel, a native of this region.**

Marine mammals are much better represented. The most commonly seen are the New Zealand fur seals which were hunted to the verge of extinction during the 1800s. With protection they have flourished and although a number get drowned every year in trawl nets they still seem to be increasing in numbers. When conservation groups have nothing better to do they raise the bogey of seal extinction because of fishing practices.

However the industry is cleaning up its act, despite a shocking 1993 season, and much of the credit is due to pressure groups. Yet fur seals still seem to increase in numbers and are spreading into areas of the North Island from which they have been absent for 100 years.

If you want to visit a colony, the one at Cape Foulwind just south of Westport is probably the most accessible, but there are many haul out and breeding spots along the coast. Knight's Point and Arnott Head host reasonable numbers. There is a certain etiquette that should be observed while around a seal colony. Stay low; you look less threatening that way, and try not to block off seal access to the sea. A frightened seal galloping towards the water is no respecter of personal space and you could get injured. They can turn up in the most unlikely places. A rubber raft group on the Mohikinui River north of Westport saw one some 30 km up the river.

Sporadic visitors include Hooker's sealions, probably the world's rarest sealion, and the sleek and streamlined leopard seals. Every now and then a misguided southern elephant seal will haul out for a while. These are usually young males which are incapable of winning and maintaining a harem. They apparently retreat to the beaches for a rest and a sulk.

Whales and dolphins, with one exception, are rarely seen from the coast. The exception is New Zealand's smallest and only endemic dolphin, Hector's dolphin. These cute grey and black animals with the distinctive dorsal fin sometimes penetrate up the larger rivers. They can occasionally be seen feeding on fish on the seaward side of the Grey River bridge in Greymouth. On calm days they often turn up off the Punakaiki coast. With the short distance involved it could easily be the same pod. Hector's dolphins are apparently threatened by set nets and many drown in these.

Kiwa Sea Adventures offer a first hand opportunity to make the acquaintance of Hector's dolphins, fur seals and spotted shags. They operate two 4.3m rigid hulled inflatable Naiads from Pororari beach at Punakaiki. The trips take in the grandeur of the rugged Paparoa coastline and give visitors a totally different perspective from that of the landbound traveller. In summer a highlight is the spotted shag nesting colony at Perpendicular Point. Here, like a multi-layered wedding cake, ledge upon ledge of breeding adult shags are quite safe from any threat from terrestrial predators. Although Kiwa owners Ra and Dean can't guarantee you'll see a Hector's dolphin, the chances are still very good. Even if you don't, the scenery more than makes up for it.

THE COASTERS

"We came here 19 years ago with five children because we wanted to give them a better environment, which we did. We love the people and we love the place."

— *Beryl Armstrong, shop manager, Hokitika.*

DESPITE the grandeur of the scenery, life isn't easy for West Coasters. The region has an ageing population which continues to dwindle. The problem lies with the lack of jobs. The bright and the young leave the place looking for greener pastures elsewhere. Hopefully the advent of jobs based less on commodity prices and more on the service industries will reflect in an increase in the number in employment and stop the "brain drain".

It isn't all one-way traffic. The Coast remains a magnet for many and this is reflected in the number of artists of various kinds. We boast possibly more potters and potteries per head of population than anywhere else in the world. Two Coast potters have achieved international reputations and more are knocking on the door (see sidebar).

A quick stroll around the Punakaiki Crafts shop or the Hokitika Craft Gallery should impress you with the quality of arts available locally.

Because of the preponderance of farming and extractive industries the people tend to be physically rugged with a strong interest in the outdoors. Men look decidedly uncomfortable in ties and those who are in professional positions have usually given up ambition in favour of the West Coast lifestyle.

For many the attractions are the wide open spaces, the lower stress and the freedom to walk at night unmolested. In short the Coast exhibits an old-time set of values and does so with pride.

This is not to say that Coasters are without fault. Like many small town folk they tend to be very conservative and to resist change with a pit bull-like determination. They'll also tell you without the slightest hesitation that they are "conservationists at heart". In the same breath you'll be told that the only reason that the Coast is still so unspoiled is because of this conservation ethic. Don't believe a word of it. The only reasons that the West Coast is still different from the rest of New Zealand are that the climate is often unsuitable and much of the land is too steep for farming. The extraction of gold, timber, coal and sphagnum moss has depended upon market price. As long as the market is buoyant Coasters will harvest all resources to the limit of their ability. Few Coasters will ever turn down an extra kilogram of whitebait.

In many ways this attitude that nature is there for us to exploit is slowly beginning to loosen its iron grip. In general Coasters still lack a strong conservationist ethic but they are grudgingly beginning to admit that conservation has some advantages and that they must move with the times.

Having said that, Coasters have a legitimate grievance towards central government. The right wing dogma of user-pays, selectively applied as always,

(Top) **"Antigravity" device at the Hokitika Whitebait Festival.** (Lower) **Kids will be kids: summertime swimmers in the Grey River.** (Left) **Barry Wilson, manager of the Hokitika Glass Studio, shapes one of his creations. Visitors are welcome to watch him at work.** (Overleaf) **Derek Sanctuary producing Westland Tweed on a 100-year-old loom.** (Insets) **The wools are first wound onto spindles. Scots tartans are among the products.**

THE POTTERS

CLOSE TO THE GOOD EARTH

(Above) **Ngakawau's John Crawford working on one of his minimalist sculptures.**

THE Coast seems to attract individualistic potters. A quick flick through the phone book shows them to be widely distributed. The reasons for their presence are not hard to fathom. It's hard to create something as elemental as pottery in the middle of a city. Many potters need space, the colours of the bush and the earth, not the tarmac and concrete of cityscapes.

Not surprisingly, there are as many different styles of pottery as there are potters. Two people in particular, Chris Weaver and John Crawford, have forged international reputations. They are quick to acknowledge that this is partly a result of having the right piece at the right time.

Chris Weaver and his family live at Kaniere, south of Hokitika. Chris likes to make functional objects rather than works of art, although he tends to the point of view that the two are not mutually exclusive. He recently achieved a string of awards including the national prize at the Nelson Potters' annual show and the national award at the New Zealand Society of Potters' Auckland Easter Show Exhibition.

These awards were won with teapots inspired by the old flat-irons belonging to his grandmother. Chris mated the pot with laminated rimu handles which he makes himself. The combination of glowing wood and rich earth tones in the pots is immensely satisfying. He also makes a range of large display pots which have a Japanese feel to them. Finished in pastel tones, they contrast markedly with the relatively sombre tones of the teapots.

Chris learned his trade at the Otago Polytechnic. When he first moved to the Coast he felt somewhat isolated and missed the inspiration he may have received from other people's work. He now sees the solitude as an advantage, enabling him to evolve his own unique style.

John and Anne Crawford live in Ngakawau, north of Westport. John is a Coaster who moved back to Ngakawau in 1974 after five years training at the Waimea Craft Pottery in Nelson. John and Anne find that the Coast gives them the space to be themselves.

John's ceramics sell as widely overseas as they do in New Zealand. He uses a variety of styles and enjoys working on his minimalist sculptures. He is still experimenting but has successfully produced recognisable horses and human figures with an absolute minimum of cues.

The Crawfords maintain a retail gallery in Westport as well as a small showroom which is attached to their workshop. John gains his inspiration from everything he sees around him, including the Crawford horse which frequently grazes around the studio. He isn't limited to pottery either and is just as happy painting or drawing.

Ceramics remain a major interest and John has hosted a seven day

(Above) **Chris Weaver shaping one of his creations in his studio at Kaniere.**

workshop for the Australian Ceramic Study Group. He has also spent time in the North Island as part of a fellowship instituted by the New Zealand Society of Potters and funded by the Queen Elizabeth II Arts Council. The intention is to allow the sharing of ideas between the two islands. A North Island potter reciprocates.

Weaver and Crawford are not the only potters on the Coast producing excellent work. Barry Paine at Nelson Creek and John Sepie from Utopia Pottery also have strongly individualistic styles. Coast potters cover a wide spectrum. If you can't find the pottery you are looking for on the Coast, it probably doesn't exist.

threatened the very social structure of the Coast. Closure of post offices and their associated savings banks in outlying areas such as Haast and Karamea placed unreasonable burdens on the local communities. The threats are not yet over. Outlying communities are being threatened with "market price" maintenance and supply fees for their electricity. Closure of hospitals has forced sick residents to travel further afield for treatment. The National Library Service mobile library will probably go soon. The list will grow longer with time.

The logic is absurd. The argument is that cross-subsidisation must be removed. Why? It is already inherent in every aspect of our lives. We have a standard letter rate throughout the country. It will always be marginally cheaper to deliver within a town than the length of the country. Should we then charge more for delivery to a house at the end of the street?

Coasters have always been political creatures but have felt increasingly betrayed by the rest of New Zealand. Certainly the Coast is New Zealand's environmental conscience and the rest of the country expects locals to look after it. At the same time central government seems to do everything it can to destroy the communities which make that care possible. No wonder Coasters are a little bitter. Blaming government for its ills does nothing but cause ulcers; kicking greenies is more fun. Times and Coasters change though.

Politics aside, the locals know how to have a good time. Social drinking is very much part of society. There are plenty of pubs to choose from and each has its own cadre of characters. There are few of the beer barns so common in the big cities. Hotel bars are similar to the English local. There is usually a fire blazing in winter and most of the regulars know one another. Most pubs contribute to a local charity and many schools have extra facilities thanks to the generosity of their pub.

(Top) **Whitebaiter in a typically reflective mood.** (Lower) **Patrons of the Tramway Tavern at Taramakau enjoying a convivial ale.**

Now that New Zealand's licensing laws have moved into the 20th century, drinking has become a lot more civilised. For 50 years from 1917 until 1967, visitors to New Zealand were treated to the unedifying spectacle of hundreds of men lined up at bars frantically pouring beer down their throats before staggering en masse into the street for the drive or walk home. This was known as the "six o'clock swill" because that was when the bar closed. Drinking after this hour was acceptable only if you were dining on the premises or were a house guest.

Coasters were much more sensible than this. While they will rigorously support any law which they believe is just, they see no point in upholding silly legislation. The result was a civilised drinking regime where a man could enjoy the company of his mates at most hours of the day or night. The local policeman who had to live in the community usually turned a blind eye, or at least until his superior officer started complaining. New police learned fast.

Leslie Hobbs in his book *The Wild West Coast*, recounts many stories of this era. In one, a bunch of 14 thirsty miners were enjoying an ale after hours when there was a knock on the front door. The landlord took his time about it but let an irate sergeant and two constables in. To the sergeant's astonishment the publican invited the men into the dining room and then proceeded to serve a minute helping of meat and vegetables to each of his guests, followed by an equally tiny portion of dessert. Then he phoned for a bus and led his guests out on what was to become a pub crawl in safer pastures.

The sergeant remained suspicious and brought the publican to court. The proprietor argued that he had invited his friends round for dinner and had provided them with a perfectly legitimate pre-dinner beer. The magistrate was undoubtedly sceptical but let the publican off. The sergeant, who suffered great loss of face in the community, decided to try again.

This time he covered all the exits with constables and then hammered on the door (scratching three times would have let him in as an illegal drinker). The publican's son answered but took his time about it. He also seemed to be hiding something. The sergeant, never a patient man, galloped down the hall towards the bar. He never made it. Someone had strung a strand of piano wire at knee height. He fell heavily and broke his collarbone. By the time the proprietor had phoned for an ambulance the piano wire had gone and the illegal drinkers had filed quietly past the sergeant and out of the only unguarded exit.

Another story recounts efforts to catch illegal drinkers at the now defunct Empire Hotel in Greymouth. Many raids were tried on this hostelry but the patrons had always left by a hidden exit by the time the police managed to get inside. On this particular night a maid spotted her boyfriend walking down the street, unbolted the door and ran after him. A raiding party arrived shortly after and the sergeant was delighted when the door opened so quickly. The police strode into the bar, notebooks at the ready. You could have heard a pin drop when they saw the local magistrate leaning against the bar, large beer in hand.

The sergeant recovered rapidly. "All boarders, I see," he announced before walking out with as much dignity as he could muster.

Coasters enjoy a good party which may be why there are so many festivals of various kinds. St Patrick's Day is always a big event on the Coast. If you don't wear something green on St Pat's day you are immediately a little bit suspect. Many hotels put on St Patrick's day breakfasts, complete with green beer.

The Coast has its own beer, Monteith's, which is batch-brewed at the Westland Breweries in Greymouth. It is shipped all over the country and trendies in boutique bars will pay a premium price for it. For a conducted tour around the brewery, contact the Greymouth Information Centre.

Coasters also enjoy a flutter at the races and the region provides a full and interesting race calendar. The most famous meeting is at Kumara and on race day this sleepy little town really comes to life (as it does for the Coast-to-Coast multi-sport event described later). In the old days a patch of bush at the far side of the track hid the horses from the punters. There are numerous tales of a horse which was leading emerging last or vice versa. Local conditions seem to suit local horses and from most meetings some Coasters come home enriched by the bets from outsiders.

Community spirit is high, if a little parochial at times. The residents of Reefton in an amazing display of unanimity managed to keep their hospital open at a time when health authorities were trying to close it. At one stage they formed a human chain around the building, which must have been one of the few occasions local Catholics and Protestants held hands in public.

So are Coasters really different from people elsewhere? Probably. They tend to be a little more generous, a little more stubborn, and more adventurous physically than folk from over the hill. They are easy people to get to know superficially, very hard to know well. They are unassuming people, happy to let you lead your life and to get on with theirs. If you are in trouble and need help you'll have a queue of Coasters to choose from. It's a great place to live and the people are the most important reason.

(Top) **A young enthusiast at Hokitika's Wild Foods Festival, 1994.** (Lower) **West Coast rugby team supporters at a home game.** (Overleaf) **The Inangahua Band playing at the opening of the Reefton Visitor Centre, 1993.**

PHOTOGRAPH OVERLEAF BY BOB McKERROW

SPORTS & LEISURE

"The place operates on West Coast time. Here in Karamea we are half an hour behind the rest of the country. It's the lifestyle; people on the West Coast have a different attitude from other people. They are less hurried, less stressed out by modern living."

— Tony Ibbotson, motel operator, Karamea.

COASTERS are sports mad. In Greymouth the most popular winter sport is rugby league, not rugby union. Just like the Coasters to be different. There is a strong women's league competition. Coasters take this totally in their stride and no-one thinks it is at all unusual that women should play this tough contact sport.

The (men's) West Coast rugby union side has such a small pool of players from which to draw that it usually finishes at the bottom of the third division.

The West Coast stunned the athletic world in 1967 when Runanga's Dave McKenzie won the Boston Marathon in 2 hr 15m 45 sec. Not only was this a race record but it was the fastest time ever run in the United States. Dave was not allowed to wear the traditional New Zealand black singlet and silver fern as he was not officially representing his country. Instead he wore his Greymouth Harriers singlet emblazoned with a large red G. Dave buried his fancied Japanese opposition on the early hills and finished the job on Heartbreak Hill before galloping through the tape several minutes ahead of second place. Officials did not know who he was. They thought the G stood for Greece. Dave still runs with the Greymouth Harriers, but because of ongoing injury problems, not at top level. After many years of tough competition, he is now a social runner.

Westport organises one of the best and most scenic road races in the country. Both the marathon and half-marathon events start in the Lower Buller Gorge. The full course takes runners up the gorge to a turnaround point. The half-marathon takes them straight into Westport which hosts one of New Zealand's best after-race functions. If you run it, get the whitebait sandwiches quickly as they disappear fast.

The beach near Kumara is the unlikely start for New Zealand's most famous multi-sport event, the Coast-to-Coast. Entrants in the one-day event bike, run and paddle their way over the Alps to the Pacific Ocean in the Christchurch beach suburb of Sumner. For those with slightly less masochistic tendencies there are two-day and team events as well. While there are now many other equally tough multi-sports events in New Zealand, the Coast-to-Coast still remains the "one to do".

The Kaniere scenic triathlon, one of the largest in the country, attracts entrants from all over New Zealand. It is usually held in March, a week before the Wild Foods Festival.

For those not into competitive sport, the Coast provides a wide range of choices. You can paddle canoes on many of our rivers, lakes and streams, often amongst awesome scenery. If you thrive on adrenalin you have a choice between

(Above) **Parapenting near the Point Elizabeth Track, Greymouth.** (Left) **Canoeists on the Pororari River. Canoes can be hired from Pororari Canoe Hire near the Punakaiki Motor Camp for adventures in the Paparoa National Park.**

NATURE TOURISM

THE ULTIMATE THEME PARK

(Above) **Massive rimu beams support the weight of The Last Resort's sod roof. Timber for the buildings was salvaged from the forest floor.**

BECAUSE nature tourism is in its infancy on the West Coast, the type and character of options is still evolving. At present most nature tourism (pretentiously called ecotourism) is still carried out by tour operators, some of them from outside the area. However there are two West Coast establishments which offer packages for the nature lover.

The Last Resort is in Karamea at the northern end of the Coast. Owner-manager Tony Ibbotson brought his fishing boat into the sleepy township to shelter from rough weather and stayed for several months. During this enforced period ashore he fell in love with the area.

Later, during a tramp on the Heaphy Track (which starts just north of Karamea), Tony realised how wonderful it would be to have comfortable accommodation designed to cater for nature tourists and trampers.

Thus began a major undertaking for the Ibbotson family. They started by salvaging timber from the forest floor in previously milled forest. The innovative design called for insulation-filled concrete panels and 480 of these were cast at the rate of two a day for 15 months. As each panel weighed approximately 320 kg, manoeuvring them into position was a major undertaking.

Cement for the venture came from the Cape Foulwind cement works near Westport. Shingle came from Granite Creek, Karamea. Local labour was used throughout. The emphasis is on energy efficiency so all the windows are double-glazed and the roof is covered with sod. As well as providing excellent insulation the sod covering serves to eliminate rain noise, a major problem with iron roofs.

The rimu beams are a massive 400mm by 400mm and the main beam in the lounge is 14m long. This was needed to support the weight of the sod roof.

After two years of construction the resort opened in May 1991. In 1992 the budget accommodation was supplemented with ensuite units which were conventionally constructed, although also with sod roofs.

Tony and his wife Raewi take great interest in the natural attractions of the area and both speak knowledgeably about these. The resort runs tours to such attractions as the Oparara Arch and to the Honeycomb Cave complex. Tony has the guiding concession for these caves and regularly takes house guests through them.

The Last Resort is licensed and has full restaurant facilities. In keeping with Tony's "buy local" philosophy most of the wines come from Nelson. When he isn't guiding, working on the resort or acting as barman, Tony is in the kitchen cooking. Amongst his other talents he makes a mean chocolate chip muffin for their guests who travel from all over the globe to the aptly named hideaway.

At almost the other end of the Coast, in the South West New Zealand World Heritage Area lies Lake Moeraki. Nestled into the bank of the Moeraki River is Wilderness Lodge Lake Moeraki owned and operated by biologist Dr Gerry McSweeney and teacher Anne Saunders.

Gerry used to be Director of the Royal Forest and Bird Protection Society, New Zealand's largest environmental organisation. Fittingly it was Gerry's Society which was largely instrumental in having the area proclaimed a World Heritage site. Few people know the local rainforest better than Dr McSweeney, who has spent 20 years working in these forests.

They set up the lodge in 1989 and have since added eight deluxe suites and upgraded the other units. Today it is now a luxury lodge with fabulous views over the Moeraki River.

Anne does most of the cooking with a team of chefs and produces hearty cooked breakfasts and cordon bleu evening meals, based where possible on local ingredients. The ambience is one of relaxed friendliness and the staff are unobtrusive and helpful.

(Above) **Gerry McSweeney of Wilderness Lodge Lake Moeraki shows a koura (native freshwater crayfish) to a group of guests during one of his noctural rambles to see glow-worms.**

What makes the place so special are the guided tours with Gerry and his staff. During July to late November Monro Beach and other secluded beaches nearby host Fiordland crested penguin colonies and seals are present throughout the year. The walk to the beach, along a Department of Conservation track, passes through some of New Zealand's tallest lowland rainforest.

Most evenings interested people are guided to feed tame eels. These giant longfinned eels will actually come out of the water to be fed. After a leisurely dinner there is often an illustrated talk on some aspect of the local ecology and a walk to see glow-worms, whistling frogs and freshwater crayfish.

The lodge has a fleet of canoes and a guided canoe trip on either Lake Moeraki or down the river to the sea is a highlight for many guests.

From April to November, Gerry and Anne organise special wilderness weeks which take guests on day trips to other parts of South Westland. Lodge staff can organise visits to any of the South Westland attractions.

It goes without saying that Wilderness Lodge Lake Moeraki operates on "environmentally-friendly" principles. It generates its own power from a mini hydro station and separates out paper, plastic and other wastes for recycling or composting where possible.

Although they operate at different ends of the nature tourism spectrum, both The Last Resort and Wilderness Lodge Lake Moeraki provide opportunities for memorable experiences in the West Coast bush.

(Top) **A visit to the white heron colony includes an exhilarating high speed jetboat ride on the Waitangiroto River.**
(Above) **The West Coast rugby team doing battle with a side from over the hill.**

rubber rafting, jet boating, skiing, mountaineering, potholing and abseiling.

If you want to mix your sports you can do so in a number of places. One company, Wild West Adventure, offers journeys through caves near Greymouth. These trips give a combination of walking, inner tube rafting, nature watching, and full-on adventure caving.

At Charleston, Norwest Adventures offers black water rafting. This piece of inspired lunacy requires the thrillseeker to don a wetsuit and carry an inflated inner tube into a cave system and float on it through a subterranean stream.

Variations on this theme exist. At the Franz Josef Glacier, Buller Adventure Tours offer a trip in which you can indulge in a visit to a rainforest, step out onto the Franz Josef Glacier and then rubber raft down the Waiho River.

Those who wish to try the ultimate in rafting adventures can try wilderness thermal rafting with Wilderness Helirafting. You are flown by helicopter to the headwaters of the Wanganui River near Harihari. The trip includes a glacier stop on one of several glaciers along the route. The rafting is exciting as the Wanganui is a grade five river. There are thermal pools on the Alpine fault and rafters can relax with a glass of champagne before tackling the rest of the river.

Another trip which requires helicopter access is up the Karamea River. This is widely recognised as the most challenging river to raft in New Zealand.

If you are into cross-country skiing, glacier skiing, mountain climbing or any other alpine activity, then a visit to Alpine Guides in Fox township is recommended. Here you can plan your trip with host Mike Browne over a hot coffee at the Hobnail Cafe.

Further south, around Haast, Haast Adventure Safaris offers a wide range of activities and a sunset jetboat ride up the Haast with host Allan Cron. This is a handy springboard to the whole of this vast south-west region. Allan can organise trips to a variety of destinations including the fascinating Red Hills area of desolate ultramafic rock.

Also based at Haast is a microlight aircraft. If you join the Haast aero club you can hire the plane and pilot for a flight around the district. The trip is recommended if you are curious about the perspective that height brings to the geology of the area. Enquire at the World Heritage Hotel in Haast.

Department of Conservation visitor centres are found at most of the more popular tourist attractions and are well worth visiting. The audio-visual display at Punakaiki is particularly good and there are numerous other excellent presentations.

The Department of Conservation maintains many tracks of varying difficulty and numerous huts on the more popular tramping routes. Tickets for overnight accommodation can be bought at any Department of Conservation visitor centre.

A number of companies offer horse treks. The Buller Adventure Tours centre on the Buller Gorge road will take you on a trip which packs a variety of terrain into a short time frame.

The trout fishing on the West Coast is world renowned. Brown trout grow to a good size in most of our rivers. The Taramakau and Hokitika Rivers offer the occasional quinnat salmon and there are also resident populations of this species in lakes Kaniere, Mapourika, Paringa and Moeraki. Check with the West Coast Fish and Game Council in Hokitika for information about licences and local regulations. The Lake Brunner Lodge at Mitchells provides luxury accommodation and expert fishing guides. It is based on the old Mitchells Hotel and was upgraded by partners Ray Grubb and Marian van der Goes. In just a few years this establishment has forged an international reputation.

The Fish and Game Council can also give you information about hunting. The West Coast has a reasonable population of deer (both red and fallow), wild pigs, goats and chamois. A number of birds can also be hunted. Any shooting of the introduced mammals is to be encouraged as they all have a negative impact on the environment.

If your interests are a little more cerebral there are always visits to the Karamea Museum, Coaltown in Westport, Shantytown near Greymouth, the Black's Point Museum near Reefton, or the West Coast Historical Museum in Hokitika. Even if you are not particularly interested in history you may be entertained here for hours during any particularly wet spells.

If you enjoy playing cards, you can attempt a uniquely West Coast game. The New Zealand forty-fives championship is held here. This obscure game is related to euchre and was introduced by the Irish goldminers. If hearts are trumps then the five of hearts is the boss card followed by the jack of hearts. Regardless of the suit, the third highest card is the ace of hearts, called the maggie. Players in many Coast pubs will be happy to show you the rules.

There are a number of festivals to choose from. Westport holds its Whitebait Festival in October. Greymouth runs an Octoberfest which includes a thrilling series of motorcycle races on a street circuit around town. This is the only bike race in the world with bales of sphagnum moss to protect riders from injury.

The big event of the West Coast cultural year has to be the Hokitika Wild Foods Festival, held every March. If ever an event typifies the title of this book, this one is it. Coasters outdo each other with ever more outlandish food. One year a possum and pukeko paté was on sale until someone complained that selling possum was illegal. There is superb food including venison, wild pig, whitebait, salmon, eel, crayfish and other West Coast delicacies. The award-winning Stonehouse salami, made in Blackball, is readily available. You can also help judge the homebrewed beer competition if you are so inclined. In addition to the food you also get entertainment. People in period costumes are commonplace and jugglers wend their way through the crowd. In the evening a dance finishes off festivities. The "world famous" Kokatahi Band plays at many of these public occasions. They dress in traditional miners' Sunday best costume and play a wide variety of instruments.

Dining out on the Coast can be a culinary treat. The Diego Restaurant and Bar in Westport has a good reputation locally while in Greymouth both the Kings Motor Hotel and the Ashley Motor Inn operate fully licensed high class restaurants. Café Collage, an innovative "bring your own" restaurant in Mackay Street, offers an interesting menu. Highlights include the kumara and pumpkin soup and the scampi.

Hokitika has the Café de Paris on Tancred Street run by Pierre Esquilat. In his time on the Coast, Pierre has won numerous awards for his cuisine. The Tasman View Restaurant at the Southland Hotel also offers good food.

Further south, good eating can be had at the Clematis Room at the Westland Motor Inn in Franz Josef and at the Fox Glacier Hotel. In the deep south the best food is at Wilderness Lodge Lake Moeraki.

This is but a brief overview of things to do and places to visit. Enquire at the information and visitor centres if you need to know more.

BOB McKERROW

(Top) **Climbers on the summit ridge, Le Receveur, Westland National Park.**
(Lower) **Horse trekking with Buller Adventure Tours on the banks of the Buller River near Westport.**

INFORMATION FINDER

Arthurs Pass
Visitor Information Centre
Department of Conservation
P.O. Box 8, Arthurs Pass
Ph. (03) 318-9211

Fox Glacier
Westland National Park
Fox Visitor Centre
Department of Conservation
P.O. Box 9, Fox Glacier
Ph. (03) 751-0807

Franz Josef
Westland National Park
Franz Visitor Centre
Department of Conservation
P.O.Box 14, Franz Josef
Ph. (03) 752-0796

Greymouth
Greymouth Information Centre
P.O. Box 95, Greymouth
Ph. (03) 768-5101

Haast
South West NZ World Heritage
Visitor Centre
P.O. Box 50, Haast
Ph. (03) 750-0809

Hokitika
Visitor Information
Westland District Council
Private Bag 704, Hokitika
Ph. (03) 755-8322

Department of Conservation
Private Bag 701, Hokitika
Ph. (03) 755-8301

Karamea
Department of Conservation
Ph. (03) 782-6852

Punakaiki
Paparoa National Park
Visitors Centre
P.O. Box 1, Punakaiki
Ph. (03) 731-1895

Reefton
Reefton Visitor Centre
Department of Conservation
P.O. Box 100, Reefton
Ph. (03) 732-83891

Westport
Information Centre
1 Brougham Street, Westport
Ph. (03) 789-6658

General
New Zealand Tourism Board
P.O. Box 95, Wellington
Ph. (04) 472-8860
Fax. (04) 478-1736

New Zealand Adventure Centre
Downtown Shopping Centre
Queen Street, Auckland
Ph. (09) 309-9192
Fax. (09) 309-9824

SUGGESTED READING

Brailsford, B. 1981. *The Tattooed Land, the Southern Frontiers of the Pa Maori.* A.H. & A.W. Reed, Wellington. 262pp.

Dennis, A., Potton, C. 1987. *Images from a Limestone Landscape.* Craig Potton, Nelson. 118pp.

Hobbs, L. 1959. *The Wild West Coast.* Whitcombe and Tombs Ltd. 158pp.

Hulme, K., Morrison, R. 1989. *Homeplaces.* Hodder and Stoughton, Auckland. 131pp.

Latham, D.J. 1992. *The Golden Reefs.* Nikau Press, Nelson. 462pp.

McSweeney, G. 1987. *Forests, Fiords and Glaciers.* Royal Forest and Bird Protection Society. 112pp.

May, P.R. 1967. *The West Coast Gold Rushes.* Pegasus, Christchurch. 587pp.

Mobil World Heritage Highway Guide: South Westland and Haast Pass. 1991. Department of Conservation, Hokitika. 72pp.

Peat, N. 1979. *Cascade on the Run.* Whitcoulls. 126pp.

Peat, N. 1987. *Forever the Forest.* Hodder and Stoughton, Auckland. 92pp.

Peat, N. 1989. *West Coast, South Island.* G.P. Books, Wellington. 123pp.

Pope, Diana & Jeremy. *Mobil New Zealand Travel Guide: South Island, Stewart Island and the Chatham Islands.* Revised Edition, 1993. Reed Publishing, Auckland.

Potton, C. 1990. *From Mountains to Sea. The Story of Westland National Park.* Department of Conservation, Wellington. 160pp.

The Story of Arthur's Pass National Park. 1986. Editor Jane Pearson. Arthur's Pass National Park. 128pp.

CALENDAR

January	Kumara races. Buller A & P Show.
February	Coast-to-Coast Triathlon. Buller Gorge Marathon and Half-marathon.
March	Lake Kaniere Triathlon. Wild Foods Festival, Hokitika. Salmon fishing contest, Lake Mapourika.
April	Powerboat racing, Lake Kaniere.
May	Westland black petrels start egg laying.
June	Blackball mid-winter Festival.
July	Fiordland crested penguins come ashore to nest.
August	Little blue penguins start egg laying.
September	Opening of whitebait season, September 1. Berlins pig hunt.
October	Octoberfest, Greymouth. Motorcycle racing, Greymouth. Whitebait Festival, Westport. 24 hour yacht race, Lake Brunner.
November	Whitebait Festival, Hokitika. Closing of whitebait season, November 14. Buller Adventure Tours Triathlon.
December	Gt Westland Marathon & Half, Greymouth. Tube race, Buller River.

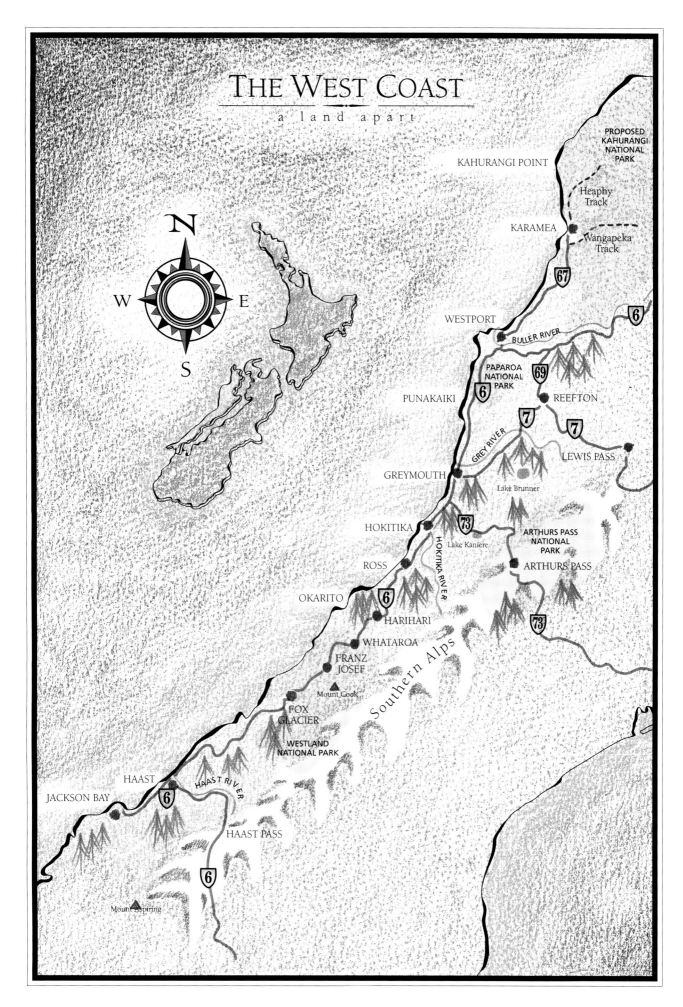

HEADING WEST

SIGNPOSTS TO THE COAST

FELICITY RYAN

> "I enjoy living here because of the lack of people
> and we're all pretty easy going. It's a fairly laid back
> style we've got and I hope it stays that way.
> Sometimes I bloody hate it though."
>
> — *Chris Cowan, Helicopter Operator, Barrytown.*